Teaching
as an
Act of Love

May. 2008

Eric,

My best always!

Richard (Mr. Lakin)

Teaching as an Act of Love

Thoughts and Recollections of a Former Teacher, Principal and Kid

Richard Lakin

iUniverse, Inc.
New York   Lincoln   Shanghai

Teaching as an Act of Love
Thoughts and Recollections of a Former Teacher, Principal and Kid

Copyright © 2007 by Richard Lakin

iUniverse books may be ordered through booksellers or by contacting:

iUniverse
2021 Pine Lake Road, Suite 100
Lincoln, NE 68512
www.iuniverse.com
1-800-Authors (1-800-288-4677)

Because of the dynamic nature of the Internet, any Web addresses or links contained in this book may have changed since publication and may no longer be valid.

The views expressed in this work are solely those of the author and do not necessarily reflect the views of the publisher, and the publisher hereby disclaims any responsibility for them.

www.thanks2teachers.com

ISBN: 978-0-595-46155-4 (pbk)
ISBN: 978-0-595-90455-6 (ebk)

Printed in the United States of America

TO KAREN

ঔৎৎ

My source of encouragement and inspiration for the past 45 years and the devoted, sensitive and loving mother of our two grown-up children, Micah and Manya, who continuously bring joy into our lives.

Contents

Acknowledgements

I've written this book in appreciation of all those teachers who gave so much of themselves to their students. From them I've learned that teaching, like parenting, is first and foremost an act of love.

In addition, I'm grateful to those parents who gave me the "gift of trust," allowing me to guide their youngsters through their formative years, as well as to the countless parents who not only supported their children's teachers in the education of their youngsters, but also contributed to the overall development of our school.

A special thanks to those teachers who have read various sections of this book and have encouraged me in the pursuit of this project: Joan Burr, Charlene Dotts-Mete, Bebe Dudley, Donna Fochi, Judy Gardner, Isabel Higgins, Connie Kapral, Edith Maclin, Mary Ann Manchester, Ann Pettengill, and, last but by no means least, Cal Rogers. Thanks also to Independence School parents Anne Alvord, Maureen Labenski and Katherine Miller.

As every principal well understands, one's school secretary is a key figure in setting the tone in the school office, assisting staff, parents and children alike and supporting the principal in the diverse daily responsibilities and minor crises that arise from time to time. There is no way I could ever adequately express the thanks due Joan Fiocchi, of blessed memory, and Phyllis Webster.

My utmost gratitude is extended to Adele Perlov who thoughtfully and sensitively copyedited the manuscript, tastefully crafting it into its final form.

And finally, thanks to Brian Mercer who designed my book's attractive and striking cover.

I expect to pass through life but once. If therefore, there be any kindness I can show, or any good thing I can do to any fellow being, let me do it now, and not defer or neglect it, as I shall not pass this way again.

William Penn

Introduction

I first walked through the front doors of a suburban elementary school as its principal in 1969, the year man walked on the moon and the year of the birth of our first child. It was the decade of J.F.K.'s "new frontier" and the Peace Corps. My mission was to provide the best possible education for each child enrolled in my new school. Seven thousand "child years" later I exited proudly through the same doors, knowing I had given it my best shot.

Those sixteen years were filled with the satisfaction of observing and guiding children through the special wonder years of five to eleven; from one step out of nursery school to the proud leap forward into middle school. I had my share of joys and disappointments, challenges and barriers, but most of all, I had stayed the course of child advocate.

I have written the short pieces in this collection over the past 35 years to inspire and give "food for thought" to all those involved with and concerned about public education—from aspiring teachers-in-training and idealistic Teach For America volunteers to seasoned professionals, from younger parents with school age children to older parents whose grandchildren are the next generation of school children. I hope my "message" will reach the educational decision makers, citizens and taxpayers throughout America who understand that the state of our local schools is second only to the family in determining the vigor and health of their communities and the nation.

Thus I invite you to join me on my journey of rediscovery back into the last millennium. This is neither a diary nor a chronology but rather kaleidoscopic glimpses through my eyes, heart and mind into the life and times of those schools and communities where I spent the better part of six decades.

When you arrive at the end of the journey, you may in fact find that it's a beginning. You alone will have to decide where you are and glean what you wish to take home with you. You, not I, will construct the particular meaning this book has for you. After all, that's what learning is all about!

LOVING
TEACHERS

One looks back with appreciation to the brilliant teachers, but with gratitude to those who touched our human feelings. The curriculum is so much necessary raw material, but warmth is the vital element for the growing plant and for the soul of the child.

Carl Jung

The best teachers teach from the heart, not from the book.

Author Unknown

Teaching as
an Act of Love

Sipping a cup of coffee in a nearly empty neighborhood mall, I noticed a young dad encouraging his youngster to crawl. Slowly I became more and more drawn into this father and son scene. I observed carefully as the infant propelled himself forward on all fours, zigzagging randomly in all directions. He was taking advantage of the luxury of a side hallway void of all moving creatures aside from his dad pushing the now empty carriage. I could sense the child's glee as he moved about on the sea of freshly polished tiles experiencing his new found freedom.

But what caught my attention was the interaction of this twosome. The father clapped in joy as his son moved towards him and then, when the child followed the carriage a few times around the lone potted tree in the middle of the hallway, he bent over laughing excitedly, and encouraged his youngster to continue on his own. All sorts of verbal and non verbal communication followed when suddenly he picked up the child, held him high above his head, then grasped him lovingly in a bear hug and twirled around in circles. Rather than put the son back in the carriage to rest, the dad put the toddler back on the floor behind the potted tree, and he began to play peek-a-boo and a modified hide and seek game, using the large planter to partially obstruct their view. When that game ran its course, the father suddenly became the Pied Piper, humming aloud and waving a plastic water bottle in the air as he marched in giant exaggerated steps enticing his son to join him in a father-son parade.

Wishing I could have caught this scene on camera, or at least on paper, I left my coffee to hurry to a nearby stationery store to buy paper and pen. Sadly for me, when I returned just a few minutes later, the father and son were gone. The potted tree stood alone in the middle of the empty hallway.

However, this brief encounter underscored my perspective on what real teaching is about. Love is the basis of all authentic teaching—both at home and at school. The dad did not follow a lesson plan to encourage his child to practice and enjoy his new found skill of crawling; the dad's motivation and sense of what was the right thing to do at the moment emanated from his heart and his relationship with his little son.

A parent doesn't need lesson plans to encourage language development during the child's early years nor to encourage the child to read, nor to do the multitude of things that children are involved in as they mature. Parenting is the natural outgrowth of a parent's love. In the same manner, teaching children in the more formal school setting is also based upon love.

Loving teachers, like loving parents, encourage students to do their best, engage them in active learning, praise children for their accomplishments, help them learn from mistakes, set limits when needed and place a priority on nurturing self confidence. Furthermore, loving teachers help their students to aim high, while creating an accepting atmosphere and emphasizing positive personal relationships and basic values of kindness, consideration, cooperation and thoughtfulness.

Without an expression of this caring, loving feeling when working with kids, teachers and their students are all left lifeless and without much meaning at the end of the day. When all is said and done, teaching must be first and foremost an act of love!

"Don't You Just Love ...?"

As the accountability movement was beginning to rear its faceless head in the early 1970s and teachers and administrators were being pressured to state their goals as measurable behavioral objectives, a cloud of oppression began to set in. The regimen of behavioral objectives resulted in more paperwork for teachers, more testing to measure these minimalist, narrowly focused objectives, and less time to pay attention to the personal needs of kids.

While some of these objectives allowed teachers to explore methods of improving their classroom program, frequently they were strictly limited to what could be measured by pencil and paper tasks. More often than not, the teachers reacted to writing behavioral objectives in the same manner as students react to senseless or uninspired homework assignments.

During one of my yearly October teacher conferences to review and approve each teacher's objectives, one 5th grade teacher walked into my office and immediately handed me a folder of her students' writings. "Read them tonight, you'll just love them." She also gave me three pages of personal and student goals, handwritten with a purple fiber tipped pen.

Thirty-three years later I still have in my possession those three pages, goals from her heart, her personal vision—not cold sterile words written on a system-wide form. Unlike most educational jargon, these visions from her heart would slowly be realized in her classroom.

These excerpts are words of a real teacher, not a technician masquerading as a teacher.

My personal goals:

"... be more sensitive to children—sensitive not only to what they learn, but how they feel about what they learn."

"I want kids to understand that we don't live unrelated to other people. We are responsible to and for one another."

"Learn to love, grow and change because man needs to be creative and sensitive."

Personal goals for students (a sampling of many):

Sam: more joyful

Dina: more responsible; caring about herself

Chris: less receptive to peer pressure

Dave: less bitter-hostile

Albert: more constructive social behavior

Katrina: not as dependent upon adult approval

Andrea: broader interests	Doreen: more responsible
Charlotte: less stimulus; more in-depth commitment	Jeff: more balanced; control temper
Shawn: learning disability pinpointed, receiving help	Ronnie: able to handle freedom, make reasonable choices

"Don't you just love" this teacher and all those others who teach from their hearts and from their love and concern for kids? Teachers who not only encourage kids to care about themselves and others, but who also inspire them to develop their skills, talents and budding interests. Teachers who refuse to be pigeonholed into boxes by school districts and by administrators who are most comfortable with uniformity and standardized predictability. Don't you just love them?

Great teachers are real people with real differences, not carbon copies; they dig down into their depths. "DON'T YOU JUST LOVE" THEM? I do.

Kids, Teachers and Curriculum

The child is the center of the educational process. Elementary education begins with the child and ends with the child. It's as simple as that!

The beauty and the challenge of the teacher's work lies within the uniqueness of each child. If teachers care for their students with love, sensitivity, and wisdom, children will thrive. Teachers will then experience the joy of witnessing students stretching to explore the world at large.

Curriculum, like a new shoe, must fit the child. It is impossible to stuff a size 5 foot into a size 4 shoe. Likewise, if you place a size 5 foot into a size 7 shoe, the child will fall flat on his or her face. The teacher must find the right match, so that the child can first walk, then run freely about with a sense of wonder, self confidence and accomplishment in the fields of study, on the playing fields, and in the wider world beyond.

If You Can Read This

I spotted this bumper sticker while driving on Interstate 81 with my family on a summer camping trip to the Great Smoky Mountains National Park in the mid-1970s.

How many other teachers would see this same bumper sticker and be as struck as I was by its simple message of appreciation. A <u>short</u> "thank you" can certainly go a <u>long</u> way!

If You Can Read This
THANK A TEACHER!

Letter from Leroy

undated
(mid-1970s)

Dear Mr. Lakin,

Hello, how is things going, fine I hope.

Tell Mr. Lyons I miss him and I improved a lot at Walden Middle School but know teacher is as nice as he was.

I miss Independence School a lot and I wish I still was there.

I hope you give another child the same enjoyment you gave me in Independence.

Yours truly
Leroy

NOTE:

Leroy was among the first group of 25 children in Project Concern[1] at our school in the late 1960s. Project Concern was a state funded program giving greater educational opportunities to inner city minority children in suburban schools.

I vividly remember Leroy. Even though he came to us in 3rd grade as a non-reader, not even knowing the alphabet, he didn't let that get in his way. With his big smile and his eagerness to learn, he realized, I suspect, that he was getting a second chance. Through the intensive and supportive help that he received from our Reading Teacher, Donna, and the P.C. Supportive Teacher, Ann Dee, as well as from his classroom teachers, he was proudly reading at a solid average level by the end of 5th grade.

I remember showing Leroy's very sweet letter of appreciation to Mr. Lyons, his 5th grade teacher—our smiles were as broad as Leroy's.

A Miracle in the Kindergarten

I never really believed in miracles until I met Kathy and Bill Casey. When their son Danny was only 20 months old, he was diagnosed with A.L.L., the most common form of childhood leukemia. A.L.L. invades the bone marrow, crowding out the healthy red blood cells.

Once the doctors had diagnosed Danny's leukemia and prescribed his treatment, Kathy Casey left her home at 6:30 a.m. every Monday morning to drive two hours to the pediatric Jimmy Fund Clinic at the Dana-Farber Cancer Institute in Boston. There, Danny bravely endured chemotherapy and radiation treatment in an effort to defeat his disease. On Tuesdays or Wednesdays, whenever the treatments were completed for the week, Kathy and Danny traveled back home to rejoin the family.

As she was a surgical nurse in Hartford Hospital, Kathy daily witnessed miracles, but now she needed her own miracle. She and Bill would do anything to prevent their gift-of-creation from slipping away. Week after week, for three years, Danny and Kathy returned to Boston to battle for Danny's life. More than enough miles were clocked to drive around our planet!

My first contact with the Caseys and their daily struggle for Danny's survival came one spring morning in

1978 when Kathy telephoned me. Ellen, Danny's older sister, would be entering kindergarten in the fall. Kathy explained that she needed to be in Boston two or three days a week. She hoped it would be less disruptive to Ellen if she attended the morning rather than the afternoon kindergarten class, thereby allowing her to play at a friend's house from the early afternoon until Bill finished teaching high school at 2:30. The school transportation department honored Kathy's request without hesitation.

Ellen entered kindergarten that fall and thrived in Mr. Hurston's magic garden of songs and play, letters and numbers, puzzles and paints. As Ellen moved up through the grades, I saw Kathy from time to time—dropping off a forgotten lunch, picking up Ellen a few minutes early or with Bill for a parent-teacher conference. Although Ellen's teachers and I were well aware that Ellen's brother was battling leukemia, I hadn't realized that Danny's treatments were only temporarily effective and that Danny was losing the fight against the 50-50 odds of surviving A.L.L.

The winter of Ellen's 2nd grade year, I received another telephone call from Kathy. Danny, although now five years old, would not be entering kindergarten. The doctors told Kathy and Bill that the aggressive chemotherapy and high doses of radiation were not working. What he really needed was a bone-marrow transplant, but neither of his two sisters had matching bone marrow to carry out a successful transplant.

However, the good news was that Danny had been selected for a test group of three children who would be given an experimental bone-marrow treatment that had recently been developed at the Dana-Farber Cancer Institute in Boston. Instead of attending kindergarten, Danny would be hospitalized for three to six months. The new treatment did not require matching bone marrow from a sibling. Instead, about five percent of Danny's own bone marrow would be removed and cleansed of leukemia cells using antibodies developed and produced at Dana-Farber. While Danny's own marrow was being treated in a laboratory, Danny would be given radiation and chemotherapy to destroy the remainder of the cancer cells in his bone marrow. The final step in this experimental process would be to transplant Danny's own cancer-free bone marrow back into his system where it would begin, they hoped, to produce healthy red blood cells.

Another year passed. I was out of school when Kathy Casey made her yearly telephone call. When I returned one late afternoon, I found a message she had left with my secretary: "Do you have room for a six-year-old kindergarten boy in September?" I thought I had understood Kathy's code—Danny was well enough to come to school. I read and re-read the message for a minute or two. Gathering my composure, I called Kathy, who told me that the transplant had indeed been a success. If Danny were healthy for another full year, the doctors would consider him cancer free. A cure for childhood leukemia was in sight and Danny was one of the first to be given a chance to grasp a lifeline.

This news was incredible. As I was hanging up the phone, I heard the night custodian unlock the outer office door. I was sure he was checking out the source of the unfamiliar sounds so late in the afternoon. I ran out to share the wonderful news with him.

Within minutes, the two of us were leaning against the reception counter red-eyed, shaking our heads in amazement. For a moment we looked at each other knowing we had just learned of our first real-life miracle.

Danny had a double dose of kindergarten, one year following the other, to begin to make up for the years he had been in treatment and deprived of a regular childhood. He had had few opportunities to be with other kids his age—to play and joke, to finger paint and draw, to chase and to be caught. Now he would be able to build with giant wooden blocks, pretend to drive a fire engine or pilot a rocket ship reaching for the moon or a far away star, or just dream and build towers until they were high enough to tumble down.

A **miracle** with a big smile and a head full of blonde hair entered kindergarten that September.

A **miracle** made possible by the millions of kids and adults who have been giving their dimes to The Jimmy Fund for cancer research in Boston since 1947.

A **miracle** made possible by years of study, research, and dedication of thousands of doctors, nurses, researchers, and technicians.

A **miracle** made possible by two parents whose love and faith in God, science, and goodness gave them and their son the strength to battle a killer without self-pity.

Every day Danny did just what he needed to do to get better. Each day, mom and dad did what they needed to do to help their son. "Impossible" was not a word in the

Caseys' vocabulary. Whomever the Caseys touched with their attitude of uncompromising optimism knew that if ever there were a kid who was going to make it, it would be Danny!

POSTSCRIPT:

I left Danny's school after his 1st grade year. Though I lost touch with the Caseys for many years, their courage and faith were never forgotten. A few years back I telephoned Bill Casey when I heard that Danny had died at 20, after having begun attending Manchester Community College. Bill explained that Danny had undergone a heart transplant as his heart had been damaged by the extensive radiation and chemotherapy treatment during those first experimental years at Dana-Farber. His body rejected his new heart, causing his death.

He shared how Danny had grown up to be a very caring and giving young man who amongst other activities loved sports and playing golf with his dad. Kathy and Bill were very proud of their son.

While the Caseys were struggling to navigate the void and pain left by the loss of a child, I sensed that the miracle of Danny would always be in their midst.

THE SENSE OF SIMPLICITY

Life is really simple, but we insist on making it complicated.

Confucius

Everything should be made as simple as possible, but not simpler.

Albert Einstein

Discovery of a Sixth Grader

I first became aware of the power of simplicity as a 6th grade puppeteer. Two friends and I, calling ourselves the Party Puppeteers, performed marionette shows for younger kids.

Once, when we were rushing to set up our portable stage frame for a performance, we encountered what we considered to be an insurmountable problem. One steel rod, from which the scenic cloth backdrop was hung, and behind which we were standing, was sagging badly. If we couldn't manage to straighten out the sag, we would be visible as we manipulated the marionette strings, thereby destroying the illusion we had worked so hard to create.

Having neither the tools nor the time to bang out the sag, we were about to give up. However, a simple solution popped into my head. Jokingly I said, "Why not just flip it over and let it 'sag up'?" Voila!

We were able to bolt the frame together with that particular steel rod now in an upside-down position. And presto—we disappeared from view and we were back in the business of illusion. "Sagging up" solved our problem!

From then on I realized that all sorts of problems could be solved quite simply by looking at them from a fresh perspective—whether upside-down, in reverse, topsy-turvy, or simply from a deliberate distance.

"Sagging Up" in Math Class

I had been attracted to my first teaching assignment in 1965 by the school district's "individualized approach" to reading instruction. However, much to my chagrin, I found out in July that I would be teaching math instead.

So I spent the next month studying the "new math" Encyclopedia Britannica Math Workshop program. As no one had given me the Teacher's Guides for the texts, and as I was too naïve to ask for them, I struggled on my own through the 4th, 5th and 6th grade books, trying to make sense of this brilliant non-traditional program. EB Math Workshop teaches arithmetic and mathematical thinking inductively using a bare minimum of words. No instructions, no examples, only number patterns, and the like, to puzzle out independently.

By the end of August, I felt that I had a clearer understanding of some of the language of mathematics (until then my least favorite subject). Convinced that I was prepared to teach EB Math Workshop, I was eager to begin with my new pupils.

At 10:00 a.m. on the first day of school in September, we regrouped for math class. My group of 5th graders sauntered into my classroom with an air of pessimism and an attitude of "try and make me learn." I thought to myself, "Oh God, how will I ever help these kids?"

These children had been grouped by math achievement levels and I had volunteered to teach the 5th and 6th grade "low" groups. The ten or so kids in each class hated math, hated school, and were humiliated by having been assigned to group "C" (everyone knew what group "C" really stood for). In fact, all of these kids did have something in common: they had all gotten lost somewhere along the way in the process of learning basic arithmetic, and had given up on the possibility of ever learning any—5th and 6th grade math "drop-outs."

So, I introduced myself. Everyone was on his or her best first-day-of-school behavior and dressed in new school clothes. I told them I needed to ask them some questions.

As I listened to their math sagas, their defeatist feelings became strikingly clear. This teacher did this, and that teacher did that, and on and on and on. They had become completely confused by the new "new math" program in the school district. (Unbeknownst to them, some of the teachers were also confused by the "new math.") Furthermore, they felt neglected in classes moving at a pace they couldn't handle.

I reassured them that their teachers did recognize how discouraged they were. And for that very reason, all the other teachers at their grade level had agreed to teach larger classes, so they could get extra help in a class of ten. Signs of relief showed on a few faces and they began to perk up.

After listening carefully to my new students and mulling it over, I decided to do something that the powers-that-be would view dimly. I completely ignored the "new math" texts and started searching in the school's storage closets for useable "old arithmetic" texts. I found plenty!

The next day I brought to class ten each of the 2nd, 3rd, and 4th grade arithmetic texts, which the kids immediately told me they had "already done." I told them we were going to do them again. But, this time they were going to understand what they "did." They smiled back as if they were thinking, "Why didn't anyone think of that before?"

Moreover, I told them that each and every one of them was going to move through the texts at his or her own pace, and that my job was to explain anything they didn't understand and to check each one's progress daily.

However, I had one new class rule. And this was the clincher for which I am indebted to my sense of simplicity and "sagging up." HOMEWORK WAS FORBIDDEN!

They had been assigned math homework every night since 2nd grade and obviously it hadn't helped them. We were going to study math at school only. Even though practicing multiplication tables and doing rows and rows of "gozintas" had been a time-honored tradition, we were going against a tradition that hadn't worked—for them.

They left the classroom surprised and shocked! Who was this crazy man teacher anyway?

Math classes began to fly by. We studied the texts and played math games of all sorts—relay races to solve computation examples on the chalkboard were the unanimous favorite. The children were beginning to see for themselves that they were progressing and had begun to take pride in their work. They were happy, I was happy, their parents were happy, the principal was happy and even the knowledgeable down-to-earth school district Coordinator of Math appeared pleased when she entered the classroom. (I think she pretended that she didn't see the verboten traditional texts and, furthermore, the kids had covered them with jazzy jackets—possibly to hide them from their more advanced peers.)

A most unexpected turn of events occurred sometime during the second month of school. One of the children asked me—no, more correctly, begged me—if he could please take the arithmetic book home and do homework.

Immediately I said "no." Rules are rules. All the others jumped in and pleaded to be able to do homework. Finally I relented—on one condition. They could take homework home only if they worked hard in class on that particular day. They reassured me that this would be no problem (which it never became) and that they would not start fooling around and performing outlandish antics as they had done in previous years.

A teacher's dream come true—kids begging to do homework, to learn more!

The year ended with all but two of the children moving ahead a minimum of a year and a half in arithmetic skills and understanding. The two exceptions were children who were identified in the spring of the year as having particular learning problems requiring specialized teaching techniques and modified expectations.

As we parted at the end of the school year, the looks on their faces and their body language were evidence that they felt differently as learners and had more confidence in themselves in general. And, of course, they had a better grasp of one of the three "R"s.

Peggy, one of my former 5th grade students, made a point of visiting me every few years and updating me on her life. Eighteen years later, when I left the school district, she stopped into my farewell party to wish me luck and to remind me again about our 5th grade math class. She had just recently entered her chosen field of nursing and was filled with pride. So was I.

The Secret of "Sagging Up"

When you care enough, simple solutions to the little and big problems fall into place. Whether it is a technical problem in a marionette show you lovingly created with your own hands, or working with children who have lost the trust in their own abilities to learn, simple solutions are within your grasp. And simple solutions are workable and manageable.

Step aside, see the humor in the situation (even if it's dark humor), use your basic intuition and common sense (be sure to logically examine the validity of your thinking), and a problem that may have seemed insolvable will be within your grasp.

But, first and foremost, lead with your heart.

Another Simple Solution

Imagine a group of 1st graders lining up to go to music class. Invariably, four or five of the kids, usually boys, are scrambling to be first in line—pushing each other and those in front of the line towards the back.

Along comes the principal with his Pied Piper "sag up." I simply walk to the back of the line and quietly direct everyone to turn around. The front is now the back, and the back, the front. From the looks on the momentarily bewildered faces of those formerly in front, I know the message of fair play has registered. And like the Pied Piper, I peacefully lead the children down the hall to music class, where they sing like angels.

SENT DOWN

1949 : Sheridan and Miss Mildred Walker

Sheridan wasn't too with it. He was the only 6th grader in our class sent down to Miss Walker's office during that entire school year. Being sent to Mildred Walker was one step removed from standing before a firing squad. What furies might be lurking in her dark chambers, hidden behind the oak paneled wall beyond her secretary's desk? No one knew.

Sheridan had been too long in the boys' room where the janitor found him juggling wet paper towels off the dripping ceiling. Immediately he was marched down to Miss Walker. Poor Sheridan, not to be seen again until the next day, too dazed to tell us what happened in THERE with HER. We never found out.

As we adored our 6th grade teacher and we wouldn't want to disappoint her, misbehavior was rare. Once or maybe twice a month, though, someone was sent into the hall. That unfortunate one prayed to almighty God that a short, stern, stocky woman by the name of Mildred Walker would not walk by.

Luckily, the 6th grade rooms were tucked away in an annex around the corner from the main hallways. The chances that Miss Walker would see you while on her daily tour of the school were slim. If she caught someone standing outside the classroom door, she would send him right back inside after a stiff reprimand.

Even though our knees shook as she spoke, her bark was worse than her bite. There were times when she even seemed human to us kids—speaking softly to our teacher or to a parent she met in the hallway.

Nevertheless, we were terrified of her and avoided being "sent down." Who knew what she could do to you when just the two of you were closed in there alone together?

Poor Sheridan knew—if he ever recovered. He moved away after 6th grade to places unknown. It remains his secret to this day.

The Late 1960s

Twenty years later, Miss Walker retired to her native Maine to care for her 94-year-old mother. Admired as one of New England's most progressive elementary educators in the 1930s, 1940s, 1950s, and 1960s, she would be long remembered as a person who cared about high standards of behavior and achievement, and who valued each of her students as someone special.

Freedom didn't mean you could do any damn thing you pleased, wherever and whenever you wanted. Homelessness and crack were not in Mildred Walker's scenario of a free country. Responsible, productive, informed citizens were her vision.

We kids of course did not understand this vision; we only knew Miss Walker's strict exterior. The parents, however, knowing the other Mildred Walker, raised enough money to present her with a new 1967 Plymouth upon her retirement. It replaced her familiar twenty-year-old black Dodge Coupe and was probably the only secret kept from her during her thirty-seven year career. The clandestine operation to raise the money was a labor of love; it felt so good to be able to bestow even a small token in return for all she had given.

On a hot and humid New England July day, she drove north, returning home to Maine in her blue Plymouth, with the dignity befitting a woman of her stature. She was justly proud of her achievements, but heavy in heart at having left behind those she had loved and tended.

ON THE LIGHTER SIDE

Substitute Teacher

One fine spring morning in the early sixties in a school near my mid-western university, a very charming school secretary greeted me—a 5th grade substitute teacher— and directed me to my classroom. I found the room and made myself comfortable at the imposing traditional oak desk.

I opened the top desk drawer and, as expected, the grey lesson plan book was awaiting the substitute. Anxious not to be unprepared for the 25 or so children soon to arrive, I quickly looked over the plans for the day:

Monday, May 18th

9:00	Opening
9:10	Reading groups (see texts on reading table)
10:20	*Spelling for Today*, pp. 189-191

I skimmed over the rest of the day, until I reached:

2:15   Social Studies, *Our America*, pp. 20-23.

It struck me that, although it was mid-May, the class was only on page 20 of the text. Wasn't it rather strange to be teaching the beginning of the basic text near the end of the school year? So, being a curious neophyte, I decided to ask the class why.

Social studies time rolled around quickly as it was a fun, cooperative class. So I popped the question. "Oh!" one child responded proudly, "We finished it! So we're doing it again!"

Indeed, the 5th grade mandated social studies curriculum in this state was *Our America*. If once through was good, twice through must have been better!

How absurd!

To Intervene or Not to Intervene

That is the Question!

As part of my M.A studies in the social sciences in the early 1960s, I was involved with a research project carried out by the Institute of Social Research at the University of Michigan. I was assigned the task of conducting "non-participant observation" focusing on the spread of change within the staffs of two elementary schools—one large and one small—administered by the same principal.

Basically, "non-participant observation" involved sitting on the sidelines of the classroom or staff meetings and ticking off predetermined behaviors that the researcher was studying. I could not speak with the teachers while I was in the class nor could I discuss the study at any time, with them or with other staff members.

However, observing and notating the interaction of children, teachers and the principal throughout that 4-month period honed my skills of observation, which served me well in later years as a teacher and principal. At the same time, I grew to appreciate the challenging and important work that was transpiring in front of my eyes. Although I have since forgotten the names and faces of those very dedicated professionals in the Ann Arbor Public Schools, I will always be grateful to them for unknowingly encouraging me to follow in their footsteps.

One observation that has remained with me for more than 40 years occurred shortly after the lunch break in the classroom of a rather inexperienced, meek 1st grade teacher. I entered the back of the classroom, sat down quietly, and tried not to attract any attention to myself, never guessing what would follow.

This teacher regularly began the afternoon with a Show and Tell session, thereby letting the children settle in and calm down after an active break outside on the playground. The first three or four children came to the front of the room, as the teacher sat relaxed and cross-legged by the side of her desk, and shared routine objects such as a new Matchbox car, a super ball or a Barbie. The other children and the teacher reacted politely although rather unenthusiastically.

Then a short freckled boy came to the front to relate how he had seen a ghost in his dream the night before and woke up crying. The teacher made an empathetic, reassuring comment and he walked happily back to his desk. More hands shot up in the air, all boys, eager to show and tell. The next boy came to the front telling, with a big toothless smile, how he had seen a real ghost in his house the night before. The teacher, not knowing exactly how to react, smiled and sent him on his way back to his seat. That ghost triggered their 7 year old imaginations!

More hands flew up into the air, waving madly. The next ghost had a knife sticking out of his belly and the teacher plainly did not know how to respond, so she quickly called upon another child. His ghost had bloody hands (obviously from the knife in the bloody belly). The teacher was turning ghost white herself as well as becoming semi-paralyzed (possibly because she had a 23 year old graduate student observing in her classroom). Not knowing how to react, she called upon a girl who could be counted on to change the subject, but as she had nothing to say today, all she could add was that she had seen a ghost with bloody legs.

At this point I should have had enough tact and courtesy to leave the room, but I didn't. The hands were now flying and in an effort to stop the bloody ghosts from completely ruining her afternoon and day (the class was now in a total uproar), she called on one "final" child. I sat there mortified for the teacher and trying to send a message to the child via ESP, willing him to tell about his fishing trip with his uncle or something akin. But no— his ghost had bloody tits. God no!

Anarchy almost overcame the classroom. The teacher was on the verge of tears, if not hysteria! I didn't know how to exit the classroom without embarrassing her more. Finally, though, I extricated myself leaving her with the bloody ghosts.

What struck me shortly after observing those bloody ghosts spiraling that classroom out of control was the realization of the importance of knowing whether and how to intervene. The teacher clearly had no notion of how to take control and intervene, just as I hadn't known how to disengage from the impending chaos.

As teachers and parents, these decisions are not always easy to make in the course of our pupils' and children's day, nor in their lives. They take careful thought. During the past 40 years I have attempted to be sensitive as to when to encourage, when to say "no" and when to grit my teeth.

For this valuable insight and lesson, I owe a debt of gratitude to the ghost with the bloody tits!

The Christmas Rooster

Grasping a jar filled with chicken feed in one hand and a leash attached to a feisty Rhode Island Red in the other, I fell totally exhausted onto the nearest chair by the classroom doorway. I sat there, sprawled out and semi-dazed, looking at the chaos of the aftermath of my first class's Christmas party 40 years ago.

Only moments before, my 6th graders had rushed sprinting and bobbing down the hallway in high spirits to board the school bus which would drop them off for their Christmas vacation. As I began to regain my senses and a degree of strength, I wondered how I could unravel myself from this predicament.

Putting the classroom back in some semblance of order would be manageable, but what in the world would I do with this rooster? I had been intending to head home immediately after the kids left, planning to rest up from my first few months as a new teacher and, especially, to recuperate from the past few weeks of excitement and school-wide festivities leading up to the Christmas vacation.

The red and green construction paper chains lying in piles on the floor in front of me had been my first introduction to a public school's pre-Christmas flurry of activities. Call me Scrooge, but once I realized that a small group of girls had gotten permission to stay inside for morning recess the whole previous week for the sole purpose of opening up a decorative paper chain production line, I put my foot down and brought the production line to a grinding halt, albeit too late. Nearly the class's entire allotment of green and red construction paper for the year had already been stapled together into enough loops to wrap the classroom in Christmas chains twice around.

I called a class meeting and proposed that the class think seriously about doing something more positive for the Christmas season than cutting and stapling paper loops. Suggesting some form of community service, I was quite indignantly informed that the Girl Scouts had already visited the homes for the elderly and the Boy Scouts had spent the previous Saturday afternoon picking up trash in the center of the town. One eager young lady then proposed that we do Secret Santas. Not being of the Christian faith, I must admit that the only Santas I had been familiar with were the ones in the department stores and those that came down chimneys. (Years earlier, I, a little Jewish boy, had secretly prayed that one such Santa would miraculously slip incognito down our chimney and leave at least one big Chanukah present.)

I confessed that their Jewish teacher had no idea of what Secret Santas were; however, when the idea was explained to me, I thought it a grand one. Little did I know that it would result in my being left bewildered, holding a homeless rooster on the eve of the school vacation, in an otherwise deserted school.

Once I understood the concept, the kids insisted we begin then and there. So I cut a piece of scrap paper into 25 or so pieces. We emptied out a wastebasket and the children dropped their names in so they might choose the name of the classmate who would be the recipient of their kind deeds for the full week leading up to Christmas vacation. I also dropped my name in.

While the class was not a cliquey one, there were a few children who were on the fringes of the group. I was secretly hoping that some of the higher status kids would by chance select the names of those who tended to be left on the sidelines, especially Regina and Jimmy.

The kids became very excited about doing good deeds anonymously for another classmate, and appeared to be even more enthusiastic about buying a gift for that person for the Christmas party. While this was in the mid sixties when the "shop till you drop" mentality had not yet swept through the country, even then kids were more than eager to go shopping down town. Being an outsider myself, and also being one who thought Christmas was becoming overly commercialized, I insisted that the gifts be made or created by the Secret Santas. My decree was not received with great enthusiasm but as the week wore on, I could see that the idea had caught on.

I overheard kids whispering to friends about the surprises they were making at home—a paperweight with artificial snow, an illustrated diary, tie-dye shirts (very popular), a hand puppet, cigar box guitars, walkie-talkies and the like. Some of the children checked with me about the appropriateness of their gift ideas. When one boy suggested a grave stone rubbing from the 18th century graveyard only 30 yards beyond our classroom windows (the art teacher had introduced rubbings during a town history unit of study), I directed him towards something more cheery.

As creative and thoughtful as their gifts were, their kind deeds were even more so. Great pain was taken to conceal the identity of the givers. Pencils were secretly sharpened, classroom jobs were all miraculously done by elves, snacks and sweets were found waiting in one's desk or locker, encouraging notes were slipped into unsuspecting coat pockets, help was forthcoming from a multitude of directions, be it with forgotten homework assignments, accompanying someone to the nurse's office, or recommending a great Newberry Award book to read for an upcoming book project.

On the day before Christmas vacation, the children trickled into the classroom from the morning buses. An air of anticipation permeated their every word as they entered laden with bags of party goodies, struggling to keep their freshly wrapped Secret Santa gifts intact. I, the official greeter, was standing by the door when one of the stragglers, Jimmy, immediately caught my attention. Being the grandson of a New England poultry farmer, I instantly spotted the Rhode Island Red that he was leading behind him with an improvised rope leash. When I asked Jimmy in a soft voice why he had brought a visitor to school on that very hectic day, he caught me off guard replying, "Mr. L., it's my Secret Santa gift!" I must have looked a little dubious. He explained that Red was one of his dad's chickens that he had fed each morning before school for a long time now, that it was something he had done by himself—a Secret Santa gift he was very proud of and rightly so. The neediest child in our class had come up with an ingenious, thoughtful, personal gift for Christmas.

Later in the morning I took Jimmy aside and asked him to tell me who would be the recipient of Red. When I heard that it was Craig, I knew a change in plans might be in the works. So I called Craig's mother during lunch and explained the situation. My gut feeling told me that Mrs. Wolf would not be enthusiastic about a rooster running around her freshly carpeted 10 room new home in a picturesque wooded section of our rural/suburban town. She couldn't have been sweeter or more understanding but there was no question of the rooster roosting in the Wolfs' home. She suggested that another student might have a backyard shed or small barn and might like to take the rooster home for the holidays.

Being realistic, I knew I would have no takers for Red and would have to come up with another plan. Amidst the confusion of the day, I was stymied. I certainly didn't want Jimmy to have his gift rejected outright so I spoke privately to Craig and Jimmy and explained the situation. They both understood and at the same moment a solution popped into my mind. Craig and I would exchange our Secret Santa gifts at the end of the day and I would find a home for Red. Jimmy's face lit up, proud that his teacher would be taking his Red home.

Jimmy went home for Christmas with his cigar box guitar, Craig went home with a pair of hand made ear muffs intended for the teacher, and I shuffled down the dimly lit hallway with a Christmas rooster trailing behind me. I called my wife from the office and asked her to pick me up, as well as an unexpected surprise guest.

Red and I were rescued shortly after we returned to the classroom by Mr. Chapman, our school custodian. He was drawn to my room from the far end of the building by the light spilling into the hallway. Chappie, as he was endearingly called by all the kids and teachers, was a part-time farmer as well. He quickly sized up the situation and jumped in to help. Without hesitation, he took Red under his wing and home for Christmas.

That was my first and last Christmas rooster. However, the thoughtfulness and kindness that the Secret Santas and Christmas Red inspired continues to be remembered to this very day, a few days before Christmas 2005.

For those still wondering, Red did not become Christmas stew.

Where is Michael Young?

Picture this: You are a "crackerjack" 2nd grade teacher. It's the late 1960s. You have twelve years of teaching behind you. Your very first pupils are approaching their twentieth birthdays.

This year you have only 22 in your class—really a very manageable number, allowing you to give lots of individual attention, except that the twenty-second student is Michael Young and Michael is like having another ten pupils—constant motion. He never stops moving in his chair or around the room. He cannot sit still long enough to get any work done or to pay attention to whatever you are explaining.

You are deeply concerned that Michael is not progressing. He's already a year behind in his reading. You know that he's bright but nothing you do seems to work. He was referred to the school psychologist by the 1st grade teacher and finally in December of 2nd grade, he was evaluated. You're waiting for a meeting to hear what suggestions the psychologist might have for you. But with one school psychologist for 3,000 students you are not too hopeful. You're also concerned that the others in your class are losing out and, although they have been good-natured about Michael's shenanigans, they too are beginning to lose patience with him.

A meeting is finally called to share the psychologist's findings; it is now almost Valentine's Day! The psychologist summarizes her evaluation of Michael, describing him as "bright" and "hyperactive." (So what else is new? Did you need to wait half a year to find this out?) You've already tried most of the suggestions the psychologist outlines—teacher's intuition—but they are not enough to effect any improvement.

The most positive news is that next year, in 3rd grade, the school district might start a pilot program for kids like Michael by providing a special education teacher to give them extra help. Terms like "specific learning disabilities" are just beginning to be referred to in the medical and educational journals. You are completely unfamiliar with this new field. All you know is that you're at your wit's ends with Michael, and if you have another year like this you'll seriously consider leaving teaching.

It's two o'clock on a Thursday afternoon. You've about had it with Michael. How often in one day can you send a child on errands or to help the custodian? Michael darts towards the classroom toilet in the back corner and flips over the red oak tag traffic signal—STOP. No one will open the door until it is flipped back to green—GO.

You are working with a reading group in the opposite corner of the classroom, thinking that you'll have a few minutes peace while Michael is in the lav. Little did you know! Sharon and Donna approach you holding hands.

"Teacher, Sharon has to use the lav, but Michael's been in there ten minutes and he won't come out." Sharon is bobbing up and down trying to contain herself. You see that Sharon can't wait a moment longer and send her to the toilet in the office.

You walk over to the lav. Everyone stops working and follows your every movement. You knock on the door. No response. Again you knock, but this time you ask in your pleasantest, firmest teacher voice "Michael, are you alright?" Again no answer. You open the door and the lav is empty. Where can Michael be now? The four girls sitting at the table nearest the lav insist that Michael went in but he never came out. One girl whispers to the group of four that "Michael must've flushed himself down the toilet." There is a chain reaction and everyone is repeating it over and over again: "Michael must've flushed himself down." Everyone is hysterically laughing and you walk over to the door and switch off the lights—a special signal to freeze and listen. "Michael didn't flush himself down the toilet, and now everyone please go back to your seat work."

Where can Michael be? There is no window to jump out of in the lav. You check the classroom—behind the puppet stage, in the cupboards, every possible hiding place you can think of.

You call the principal who comes immediately to check out the situation. He calls the secretary to ALL CALL the entire school on the intercom to see if anyone has seen Michael.

Ten more minutes go by. By now the principal and the custodian have checked out just about every nook and cranny in the school. No Michael Young. You are beginning to become flushed from the tension of it all. The P.E. teacher has checked the school grounds and Michael doesn't appear to be anywhere.

It's almost dismissal time. Michael Young has disappeared!

The principal calls the police department and a patrol car arrives within minutes. The officer questions you and you repeat the story. At about 2:00 Michael went into the lav and didn't come out. When the officer says that the kid couldn't've flushed himself down, the class becomes wild with laughter. You flip out the lights and everyone freezes again. The policeman gives you a look as if to insinuate you are a real loon.

You are beginning to lose your cool. The 3:15 dismissal bell rings. You dismiss your class, walking them down the hall—without Michael. What a story the kids are going to take home today! How many telephone calls will you get from parents just wondering whether their child was making up stories again and if what they had been hearing all year about this Michael Young is really true?

Having walked back in from the buses, you sit down at your desk, take a deep breath and then walk to the lav for another look. The principal is calling Michael's parents and the Superintendent of Schools. The chief of police arrives at the scene and decides to send out a search party to check the nearby woods and abandoned granite quarry.

Another hour passes and Michael is nowhere to be found. The principal and Superintendent tell you to go home, as there is nothing more you can do. If Michael is not found by 5:00, his disappearance will be announced on the 6:30 local TV news in an effort to locate him. You prefer to stay put, where you alternate between correcting papers and pulling down a Mexican bulletin board. You begin to staple up the red background for a Valentine's Day display.

In total exasperation and without forethought, you screech out: "MICHAEL YOUNG, WHERE ARE YOU? WHERE ARE YOU????" Your hands are shaking as you continue to staple the red construction paper. The school is as silent as a morgue. Then … you think you hear something above your head. You must be imagining it, maybe hallucinating. Again you hear sounds like squirrels running about in an attic.

He's—it couldn't be—he's up in the crawl space above the suspended acoustic ceiling tiles. Impossible! How could he have ever climbed up there, ten feet above the floor?

You call the principal, who calls the night custodian for a ladder. The custodian pushes up one of the ceiling tiles into pitch-blackness. The principal runs to get a flashlight. This time the custodian, using the flashlight, thinks he sees something move near one of the hidden ventilator ducts in the ceiling. You climb up the ladder with the flashlight and sure enough what looks like a turtle crawling along about twenty feet away is none other than your Michael Young.

Yes, Michael Young was not flushed down the toilet. Michael was in school the next day, but you take a "mental health" day to recover from your close encounter with insanity.

Eighteen years later, you are nursing a cup of coffee in the Teachers' Room during a short morning break when the name Michael Young catches your eye in the local newspaper.

Could the Michael Young who ran into a burning house to save a mother and two children be your Michael Young? Michael Young, where are you? Where are you?

A Rabbit on Trial

The scene of the crime

Suburban New England elementary school
Beautiful fall September morning, 1981

I am greeted at 8 a.m. by Mr. Kittle, our school custodian, who appears agitated. He invites me to accompany him to Mrs. S's 5th grade classroom where he has been chasing mice since 7:45 a.m.

Mrs. S's classroom is full of life, both figuratively and literally. Her informally structured classroom resembles both a family room (second hand carpet and couch, shelves overflowing with books) and a petting zoo dropped down into a traditional box-like school classroom amidst tables where small groups of children pursue challenging and personalized studies and projects. A child's dream, a teacher's dream, a principal's dream, a custodian's nightmare!

I head back to my office, also somewhat disturbed, to say the least, to be starting my day dealing with rabbit urine and mice on the loose. Without extending the courtesy of speaking with the teacher when she arrives for the day, I write the following brusque memo:

From the desk of Mr. L.
Date: 9/16/81
Time: 8:35 a.m.
To: Mrs. S.

URGENT

1. The couch has to be discarded because of the rabbit urine and droppings.
2. The rabbit and cage must go home today.
3. The mice must be securely covered each night as I put one of them back into its cage at 8 a.m. and Mr. Kittle is spending time each morning on his building check chasing after mice in your classroom.

A formal appeal from Mrs. S's students

Dear Mr. L. and Mr. Kittle,

We, Mrs. S's class, are very sad about your decision concerning our rabbit.

We feel we've been exceptionally good about keeping our classroom clean and that last night was an exception. It was an exception. It rained yesterday and BUN BUN was not able to exercise outside. This caused BUN BUN to be overly active during the night and soil the couch. (This is not his usual behavior.)

We are extremely sorry that this caused Mr. Kittle extra work and are willing to give up our recess time to help him with some of his other chores.

Two weeks ago we asked Mr. Harris to build a cage top and an outdoor cage. The outdoor cage is already completed and he is rebuilding the inside top because he made the wrong size. Also, we have moved BUN BUN to the glass cage. We accept our lost couch, realize that we have to use two dictionaries on the rat's cage, but feel the rabbit decision is rather harsh.

We are begging you for a trial week, to show that we can control BUN BUN. If during that week or thereafter the rabbit causes the slightest bit of extra work for Mr. Kittle, we will agree that he must leave our classroom.

Affectionately,

Tracy	Seth	Rob
Ashley	Tina	Lisa
David	Sarah	Heather
Matthew	Kirstan	George
(BUN BUN)	Carlene	Carey
Paul	Chrissy	Judy
Jason	Mrs. S.	Mike

The decision

Time: 1:45 p.m.
Date: Same day
To: Mrs. S's Class,
I received your letter and I am willing to give your class a trial week with Bun Bun.
Mr. L.

Probation officers' reports (Messrs. Kittle/ Harris/Cooper)

Trial week:

Bun Bun was kept under very close supervision during this trial week. She was held and hugged often by the kids who obviously adored her, and she received plenty of exercise in the school court yard. Bun Bun passed the trial week without any infractions. No evidence of urine stains or droppings outside of her cage!

Mid year report:

Bun Bun continues to thrive under these ideal classroom conditions, living under very hygienic conditions and showing great self control—especially relating to the replacement couch.

End of year report:

Bun Bun's classroom decorum continues to receive the highest ratings from this probation officer. A classroom lottery is being held and the 4 winners will be able to take Bun Bun home for a 2 week period each during the summer vacation.

It is also recommended by this probation officer that Bun Bun be allowed to return to Mrs. S's classroom next September and live out her natural life in this rabbit friendly and human friendly environment.

NOTES:

- After I had written the original memo to Mrs. S. I was annoyed with myself for having acted so impulsively and tyrannically. I look upon myself as a child centered and humanistic person who listens thoughtfully to others, values problem solving and weighs decisions carefully and sensitively. Even though I had acted like an oaf, I was not one bit surprised when Mrs. S. grasped this opportunity to turn the incident with Bun Bun into a real-life group problem solving exercise for her class as well as for all involved.
- The letter in the text is the original wording of the letter sent to me on September 16, 1981. I wonder what these former students are doing 24 years later in their mid 30s.

Might some of them be mothers or dads, animal rights activists or veterinarians, lawyers or policemen/women, environmental scientists or forest conservationists, computer mathematicians or hi-tech entrepreneurs, soldiers or musicians, poets or teachers, politicians or stand-up comics, graphic artists or small business persons, tree surgeons or neurosurgeons …?

I would love to hear from my former students (rlakin@ thanks2teachers.com) and learn about your life journey. Living in the Middle East for the past 21 years, I have concluded that life is as beautiful and as complicated as a Persian carpet!

SENT DOWN— AGAIN

Where to Begin?

As my elementary school principal, Mildred Walker, was ending her career, I was beginning mine. She most certainly was not the retiring head of the out of control school where I began as principal in 1968. Twenty years earlier, being "sent down" was no laughing matter. Today it was.

I wasn't prepared for an office full of children being sent down to the principal by their teachers. What was it going to be this time: Fooling around in the classroom or throwing bits of food in the lunchroom? Fighting on the playground or tripping someone in the bus line? Shoving an unsuspecting passerby in the hallway, or switching the contents of two distant lockers unbeknownst to their frantic users? And on and on and on—and all clearly the expected and disconcerting results of a laissez-faire approach to children and their schooling.

Faces soon became familiar as the same three or four children were sent down from each class, with a smattering of new faces not wanting to be completely left out of the action.

How I longed for those bygone days when kids walked to their neighborhood school, back and forth twice a day, greeted at noon by moms anxious to hear about their morning at school and eating lunch listening to the latest radio serial, possibly Helen Trent, Woman Reporter or Our Gal Sunday. Kids, tired out from physical exercise when they arrived back at school, were ready to sit down and listen quietly—even if only for fifteen or twenty minutes—as their teacher read aloud from *Stuart Little* or *The Snow Goose*. No one was hyped up by a fifteen-minute, or longer, bus ride with its hornet's nest of activity.

Within days of arriving at my new school, I learned from the office staff's "discreet" remarks, made within earshot so I would certainly overhear them, that the previous principal, of relatively short tenure, was not from Mildred Walker's school of thought or action.

Children "sent down" were told by the school secretary to sit down on the comfortable vinyl couch (not the hard wooden bench of yesteryear) outside the principal's office. Within ten minutes, she would send the children back to their classrooms, as their silliness and noise were too much for her to cope with. A few were spoken to, but most were never seen by the principal. No warnings, no lectures, no listening to the kid's side of the story, no tap on the shoulder to encourage him (it was usually a him) to think before he opened his mouth the next time. Nothing said, nothing done. For the kids, being sent down to the principal was really a laughing matter.

I certainly did not think that my new situation was funny, though, as my vision of a principal was not one of judge, jailer, or probation officer. During the first months, I tried to speak with every child who was sent down. The secretary was instructed to keep the children in the office until I returned to the office—sometimes an hour or more wait, as many of my hours each day were spent in classrooms acquainting myself with the children, teachers, and curriculum.

My conversations with the children were a crash course in "everything you wanted to know about school but were afraid to ask." I tried to keep a straight face to the answers to my simple question: "Why were you sent down?"

- "I don't know why Miss N sent me down." ("OK, I'll ask her"). "Well, maybe it's cause I...")
- "I was only fooling around, I didn't mean it." ("Pulling a chair from under someone is not 'fooling around.' Do you know what a wheelchair is?")
- "I kept raising my hand and Mrs. W. wouldn't call on me. I had to go really badly." ("Doesn't your class have a lav pass?") "Yes, but Brian hid it."
- "Seth talked to me first, I was only answering his question, and he wasn't sent down." ("Go get Seth, please.") "Do I hafta? I promise I won't do it again."
- "We were just playing in the nature corner with the white mice when they got out by mistake." ("Come with me. We'll try to catch them.")

- "I told her that I wasn't talking, but she said that I've spoken to you three times today—young man, out!" ("Tell me about the other two times.")
- "The teams weren't fair, so when Brett laughed at Craig for striking out, John got mad and hit Andrew, and then Andrew hit me. Honest. That's how it all started. Really, I didn't do anything." ("OK, then, why were you sent down?")
- "We were only hiding under the desks to surprise the music teacher when she came in. She didn't think that it was funny when we yelled "Surprise!" so she sent us all down." ("So, what are you ALL waiting for? Go back and apologize.")

Talking with the kids was getting nowhere. Some days it was a trickle, other days a steady stream. But there appeared to be no end to the flow. I needed to meet with the teachers.

We sat down together. The teachers talked about their frustrations, trying to teach in a school whose pupils were becoming more and more out of control each year. Here was a group of people whose idealism and professionalism were being snuffed out by a school that seemed about to thrust itself into orbit. As elementary teachers are generally optimistic, and are dedicated to making a difference for children, we had no doubt that the children would respond positively to our steps to create a more orderly learning environment. Freedom to teach and to learn. Not freedom to disrupt, to be disrespectful, and to destroy.

I envisaged a school where learning was valued and admired, curiosity stimulated, kindness reciprocated, problem solving practiced, and self-confidence cultivated. Old habits die hard.

Where to begin?

Grant Clark

In addition to zeroing in on the curriculum and teaching strategies during my first few years, it was imperative that improving discipline throughout the school be one of my top priorities. I made a commitment to myself to follow at least one class of children through from kindergarten to 6th grade as well as to work with teachers and parents to create a more positive learning environment in the school.

I was spending countless hours dealing with those children sent down to the principal's office—a continual stream of children and a barrage of problems. If I ignored them, the teaching staff would naturally doubt that I was serious about supporting them in tackling the overall discipline problem. Furthermore, if I did nothing, the kids would continue to view their absurd antics or their friends' outrageous actions as acceptable school behavior, since there were no consequences.

Grant, it turned out, was indirectly responsible for keeping me from losing my sanity. He was a 5th grader whose behavior was becoming more out of control each day—the most disruptive student I had had to deal with up until that point.

Grant had been sent down so frequently during the week of April Fools' Day that I was about to pull out my hair. I had tried a number of times to contact his parents at home, but to no avail (this was before the advent of cellular phones).

Finally, by mid-week, I had succeeded in reaching his dad at work. I explained the details of his son's week—so far; it was only Wednesday. (I had jotted down the details in preparation for an outburst from an indignant parent at the other end of the line.)

Mon., Tues.	talking incessantly in class;
Monday noon	throwing water bombs in the boys' room;
Tuesday, 10:45 a.m.	banging on the classroom door when told to wait quietly in the hall for a few minutes;
Tuesday, 1:30 p.m.	and finally in Grant's own words, which I read to his dad: "Before we lined up to go to another class, John B. started to say 'poor Grant' a few times. Then I said 'stop it,' but he went on saying it. Then I asked the teacher if I could punch him, but she said 'no.' I said 'he is going to make me start a fight.' The teacher said 'hold your tongue.' I said 'no, I don't know how to'."

When I finished speaking, there was a lull of two or three seconds. However, I had no intention of breaking the silence as this was going to be Grant's problem, not mine! Dead silence.

Then Grant's dad, Mr. Clark, after a muffled sigh of displeasure, responded that he was in the middle of a departmental meeting and requested that I put the details I had just relayed to him in writing, and promised that he would take some action and get back to me. Fair enough! He was a busy executive.

It was 2:00. I quickly composed a letter to send home at 3:15 with Grant—hand delivered. My secretary typed it as fast as possible amidst the usual flurry of end-of-the-day telephone messages. So as not to miss Grant, I walked triple-speed outside to the bus lines. I didn't want another day to pass without intervention from home. When I found Grant in one of the long boisterous school bus lines, he was kicking another child. It is an understatement to say that he was surprised to see me appear out of nowhere. The shocked look on his face conveyed that he knew something serious was brewing. I told him to give the letter to his dad and that I had just gotten off the telephone with him, and he was expecting a letter. The shocked look deepened.

The following morning when my early bird secretary arrived at 7:30 a.m., she found an envelope marked "Attention: School Principal" sitting dead center stage on her otherwise cleared desk.

April 4th

Dear Sir:

Regarding your telephone call yesterday afternoon, let me preface my remarks with my wholehearted endorsement of your program to establish closer communications between the school and the home in matters of pupil discipline. You may be assured that we will provide follow-up action at this end.

With particular attention to the incident of April 1st, my son has related a story, which leaves a credibility gap. In order to assist me in sorting the fact from the fantasy, I would appreciate a note from the teacher containing more details of the originating incident. I do not question the equity or the necessity of Grant's discipline. These facts are merely to assist me in impressing upon my son that he is fully accountable for his actions while in school and that he cannot profit by distortion and/or omission.

Speaking as the father of three of your school's tribulations—Jeffrey, Brett and Grant—and with due respect to your wisdom and experience, I would like to suggest the following: that students sent to your office spend their period of penitence in writing a report of their misdemeanors. This report could be verified by the reporting teacher upon the pupil's return to class. Including the verified report with your report form to the parents would provide us with a more complete picture of the case. The more important benefit would be that the pupil's thoughts would be properly directed to reflection on the cause of his punishment. I do not feel that fidgeting on a chair in your office is an effective deterrent to further detours from proper behavior.

Congratulations on your new system! It is a welcome sign in a school that my wife and I have both felt to be too permissive.
Sincerely yours,
Graham Clark

While Grant's dad didn't exactly set the stage for personal contact, it was definitely an overture, and I soon followed up. A few days later, the teacher, the Clarks and I sat together in my office to help Grant become more productive and less disruptive in school. I suggested a daily report/check off sheet to be taken home nightly, signed by his dad and returned to his teachers and me the following morning. This was to be Grant's ticket to enter the classroom each morning thereafter.

The "wrath of God" approach to discipline was not the one I had wanted to foster in my new school. However, it was what Grant was accustomed to. It worked wonders, as it was very important to him to please his dad. Order and calm returned to Mrs. R's classroom—the teacher was happier, the Clarks were happier, and—after an initial period of shock—so was Grant. But I was happiest of all; Grant's executive dad's suggestion for a way out of this confusion and disruption led to my plan for: Letters to Mr. L.

Letters to Mr. L.

Deer Mistr L,

I hav a problim. I hav the runs. That's way the teacher send me down her.
Danny B.

Danny, a 3rd grader, not only had great difficulties in learning to read and write, but also was a frequent visitor to my office. His teacher had been so discouraged by his incessant talking that on this particular occasion she ignored him even though this time he was in real need. After urgently interrupting the teacher again and again, he was sent down. When he arrived in the office he immediately used the toilet in the nurse's room. The secretary, unaware of what was happening, then asked him to write a letter to me explaining why he had been sent down.

A few minutes later he dashed back into the nurse's room, but not in time. Our school nurse helped him through this most embarrassing incident, calling home for a change of clothes; she had him back in class within the hour, "smelling like a rose." (Not long after this incident, he was one of the first children to receive extra help each day from the Learning Disability Resource Room Teacher.)

Danny's letter was one of scores to be written to me by students sent down. Each child sent down was given a clipboard with instructions to write a short letter telling me:

1. Exactly why he or she had been sent down and by whom.
2. What steps he or she would take in the future to prevent being sent down again.

The younger children, learning to read and write, dictated their letters to the school secretary. Thereafter, the children sent down were constructively occupied in the school office and, upon completion of their letters, were immediately sent back to class.

I was now in the driver's seat. I could call children to my office at my convenience. Not knowing when they'd be called down to the principal's office served to build up some anxiety for those who had a real reason to worry.

Would I send their letters home for the parents to sign, or would it be only a kindly warning? Would I telephone their parents or, worse yet, would they have to telephone one of their parents from my office in my presence and explain what they had done to require such a drastic measure (such as throwing a stone at another child on the playground)?

Many children were sent down for minor reasons (and some, it appeared, for no reason). Speaking to them personally during my daily wanderings through the school would usually suffice, without having to call them down.

Other letters required more attention and direct action, such as the letter from "Jason, the Innocent."

My message was slowly getting through to the children, teachers, and parents: an orderly learning environment was to be the order of the day. Children would be challenged to learn, not learn to challenge their classmates and teachers senselessly. Freedom to learn in an orderly, not chaotic, environment would prevail.

Group Problem Solving and Conflict Resolution

Dear Mr. L.,

It's not fair. I wasn't the only won. Jhon and Scott were running after us and she saw me hitting Bret and sent me in. I'm
sorry Bret had a bad nose bleed and Mr. Kittle had to clean up
all the blud in the halls. I hope he's better.

Jason, Room 6, Grade 4

Typical of most letters from kids sent in from the playground, Jason's letter gave me little clue as to what may
have transpired on the playground. I decided to call down
all the children mentioned in his letter. Before I could
even begin, each insisted that this one or that one was
guilty of this or that. So I dispatched Jason the Innocent
to call the others in from the playground.

This was not a happy bunch. Missing their noon
recess, they gave one another the evil eye. After I asked
the enlarged group, now nine strong, to tell me in detail
what had occurred on the playground, they proceeded to
disagree on each point. Nine angry boys crammed into
my 8' by 10' office, reeling off an assortment of accu-
sations. Feeling rather exasperated and having had no

prior training in how to deal with an emotionally charged mini-mob, I walked out of my office for a moment to regain my perspective. Taking a deep breath, I went back in, ready for "on the job training"—problem solving with nine angry 4th grade boys. One boy, on the verge of tears, blurted out, "Mr. L., we can't agree." Taking my cue from him, I said, "OK, I'll leave, and when you can all agree on what really happened, call me back in." I returned uninvited a few times to check on their progress and when it became obvious that they still couldn't agree, I told them to call me ONLY when they were absolutely certain that they had "one story"—not three or four different versions. Ten minutes or so later they called me in to relate their "one story." However, just as they finished, the end of the noon recess bell rang. I asked them to return at the beginning of the next noon recess, when I'd explain what action I'd take. Oh boy!

All of the nine boys had agreed that they were about equally responsible for what had happened. It had all started when they began playing catch with two girls' hats. The boys ran after each other and the girls ran to the teacher on duty to complain. The teacher ignored the two girls because the same twosome had egged the boys on the previous day. The game of catch continued until the boys started fighting. And unlucky Jason was caught by the teacher and sent in. Like most fooling around (pushing, shoving, chasing, grabbing), it usually begins in a playful mood, leading to name-calling, an argument, or a fight, possibly an injury, and, most likely, tears.

The following noon, I explained to the boys that I would be quite lenient. It was their first time in my office and we all make mistakes, don't we? If they learned from their mistakes, fine. But if they repeated the same mistake, I would consider it to be much more serious. "Only fools make the same mistake over and over. You boys are definitely not fools!"

I had aimed for my disciplinary measures to be fair, firm, consistent, and related to the child's behavior. As they had been using the playground unsafely, being grounded from the playground for one day was the price they had to pay as a consequence. (The concept of "logical consequences," which is clearly outlined by Rudolf Dreikurs in his 1964, now classic book, *Children, the Challenge*, has guided me immeasurably throughout the years in encouraging children to become more responsible for their own actions.)

If I had to speak to them about playground problems again in the future, I explained, they would be grounded, first for three days, then four days, and so forth. As they left my office, I observed that they were beginning to understand my approach to discipline and were relieved that I didn't verbally bully them, and thankful that their new principal seemed reasonable.

What struck me most about our meeting, though, were the good feelings that surfaced at the conclusion of the sessions. No one blamed anyone; there was no undercurrent of intimidation or rage as the nine walked out of my office. In fact, the boys were planning their next noon recess, in two days, with their new-found best buddies.

"We'll meet at the 4-Square."

"No, why don't we join the street hockey game with Mr. G.? We won't get into trouble. Mr. G. has extra hockey sticks, too."

"OK, but if we can't get into the hockey game, I'll run out and get a 4-Square for us so we'll be sure to get one."

"Don't forget, we have to go to the library for recess tomorrow, or Mr. L. will add on another day."

"Don't worry, we won't forget, but remind us anyway."

"Alright, and bring D&D to the library. Maybe the librarian will let us play in a corner."

A simple system of interpersonal problem-solving evolved out of my meetings with Jason the Innocent's group of nine. (That was in the early 1970s. Today the areas of mediation and conflict resolution are further developed and widespread.) As conflicts are bound to arise in classrooms and schools, I was hoping to encourage kids to practice and internalize problem-solving skills, which they could carry with them into their teens and adulthood.

The beauty of this approach is that the children basically solve the problems themselves. You are their "guide." You do not set yourself up as judge or inquisitor. As the children don't have to prove their case, nor risk losing face with the other kids or you, it's much easier for them to be direct, honest, and, most importantly, to compromise and find a workable solution.

The process is simple. The "guide" asks ALL the children involved to sit together in a private room and to call the "guide" to join them ONLY AFTER THEY ALL AGREE upon:

- how the problem <u>began</u>;
- what exactly <u>happened</u>;
- what specific steps or action they plan to take to <u>prevent</u> the same or similar problems from recurring in the future.

This system worked so well in my school (no hundred percents; there never are with people), that my wife and I decided to try the system at home with our five-and eight-year-olds. Our children learned that we weren't going to take sides. Therefore, they didn't run so quickly to a parent to complain about the other sibling when a problem arose. However, when they couldn't solve something on their own and needed parental help, they knew they'd be sent upstairs together to agree upon both what had happened and a solution before returning downstairs. Since one or both were quite upset when they came to us (be it a battle over the television or because one was bugging the other, or ...), they realized that prolonging the emotional outburst was going to be counterproductive. They came to realize that the sooner they could regain control of themselves and speak with each other and agree upon a solution, the sooner they could get back to watch television, or to play, or whatever.

As parents, not being the judges or inquisitors made for a much more supportive relationship with our children and kept channels of communication open and not cluttered with unnecessary garbage.

Fifteen years later, when asked about our approach to problem-solving with them, our young adults responded that they thought it really worked because they learned to solve their own problems and they felt that they had been treated fairly, as neither parent had taken sides.

Today, many years later, I wonder what the kids who sat in my office in the 1970s and 1980s solving their problems with their classmates learned about settling conflicts verbally and non-violently.

If among my readers is one of those who sat at my round table, or in the workroom next to my office, working out an agreement with your classmates, I am anxious to hear from you. Do you believe, as I do, that human beings can sit down and speak with one another and solve problems?

Have you been able to incorporate these skills into your life and pass them on to others? Regardless of the particular meaning these experiences have had for you, I look forward to your reply (rlakin@thanks2teachers.com). It's never too late for one's students to continue to educate their principal!

ENCOURAGING CHILDREN TO LOVE LEARNING

The man who doesn't read good books has no advantage over the man who can't read them.

Mark Twain

J. K. Rowling,
Meet Irma Conwell

Irma Conwell was at the same time a widowed mother raising three daughters on her own, and an unorthodox educational leader. A graduate of Columbia University Teachers' College in the early 1940s, she was a woman of vision, principle, dignity and charm. As the Director of Elementary Education in the rapidly growing suburban Connecticut school district where I took my first teaching assignment, she had turned the school district upside down in the 1950s and early 1960s. It was a time of severe teacher shortage and she recruited young-spirited idealistic teachers who were drawn to her quiet dynamism, to her passionate commitment to individualization of instruction and to her unwavering determination to encourage the love of reading in children.

When I arrived on the scene in 1965, the core materials of the school district's reading program were the quality children's literature in the school library. Dick and Jane were long gone—"RUN, DICK, RUN."

Those boring, banal basal readers were replaced for beginning readers by the likes of Amelia Bedelia, Clifford the Red Dog, Curious George and books of Dr. Seuss. As they progressed, the children encountered the works of a host of talented authors including E. B. White (*Stuart*

Little and *Charlotte's Web*), Beverly Cleary (the Ramona and Henry Huggins books), Marguerite Henry (*Misty of Chincoteague* being one of her many popular horse stories) and Laura Ingalls Wilder's Little House books which were adored and devoured by countless readers many years before the now classic 1970s TV series. My 5th and 6th graders delighted in such challenging Newbery Award Winning books as *A Wrinkle in Time, The Witch of Blackbird Pond, Call It Courage, Johnny Tremain,* and *Amos Fortune, Free Man.*

Each child's interests guided his selection from the hundreds of titles available on our weekly class visit to the school library. Hundreds of books sat patiently on the library shelves, ready to entice the next child walking by to be taken to the library carpet to preview its jacket and to leaf through its pages. Certain titles and authors became so popular that, at times, friends would dispute over who would be the first to take out the one in demand. Thus, the beginnings of a love affair between children and their books.

Once back in the classroom, the children would settle comfortably into their chairs and relate to their chosen ones with great interest and intensity. The written words wondrously flowed, it seemed, into their imaginations and minds.

A weekly individual reading conference was set by the teacher to discuss the books, to have a heart-to-heart about important details and developments in each child's personal book. In addition, teachers provided lessons in phonics and specific skills of reading comprehension, using a variety of teacher-made and purchased materials to strengthen the developing reading skills of the individual child and to support the readers' exploration of the people, the ideas, the cultures and the world of fantasy within their books.

One needn't have administered any standardized tests to observe the children's affection for reading and books. Listening to children read at weekly conferences confirmed face to face the child's growing mastery of vocabulary and appreciation of plot, character, mood and style. Furthermore, the children eagerly looked forward to that special time of day when the teacher read aloud to the entire class a book of the teacher's own choosing to be mulled over and relished.

Irma Conwell left our town in the late 1960s. Moving to Honolulu where she taught at the Kamehamaha School, she returned to her love of teaching youngsters and language arts. She hadn't been adequately appreciated in her Connecticut town, to say the least, as her child centered reforms stirred up too many waves and were ahead of the times. However, her passion for individualization and for fostering the love of reading took root. During my 15 years as principal I saw modifications in the reading program, yet the love of reading literature ("real books") remained at the core. Small group literary circles were added to the system of individual reading conferences while more sophisticated supplementary materials were provided to teachers to refine the reading program. Nevertheless, when I visited my former school twenty years later in 2004, I saw different children and different teachers but still abundant evidence of the love of reading.

J.K. Rowling, you arrived too late in the picture—40 years too late—to have bolstered Irma Conwell's concerted and courageous efforts in the 1950s to incorporate children's literature into the center of a school district's reading program where *Dick and Jane* still reigned supreme.

She had clearly understood and articulated the POWER of placing the right book in the hands of every child. Her championing the RIGHT of all children to become immersed in books and to acquire a "love of reading" at an early age would finally be unequivocally validated by the millions of young readers held spellbound by your Harry Potter books. Thank you J.K. Rowling! And thank you Irma!

Irma Meyer Conwell passed away peacefully on April 28, 2001, at the Arcadia Retirement Residence in Hawaii.

A Principal's 11 Tips: How NOT to Encourage Children to Read

1. Expect each one of your children to be "reading" no later than December of 1st grade.
2. Worry, worry, and then some, that your 1st grader will be a non-reader. DON'T worry about the anxiety your worrying will create in your child—very important.
3. Stop reading aloud to your child when s/he reaches 1st grade. S/he should be able to read independently by then, and furthermore only preschool children love being read to.
4. If you think your child is not making rapid enough progress in school, have your child read aloud to you for a half hour every night. Be sure to correct every mistake that s/he makes in order to improve your child's self-confidence! This is especially critical! Remember to use a tone of voice that displays sufficient disappointment when you correct each word your child has gotten wrong.

5. Remember to continually reinforce to your child that you cannot understand why s/he doesn't love to read as you did when you were a child.

6. A corollary to 5: Bring home those titles from the library that you loved as a child; only "classics" when s/he is older.

7. Insist that your child read only challenging books with many new vocabulary words on each page.

8. Discourage your child from reading books s/he loved when s/he was younger. Be careful to explain that these are "baby books."

9. When your child shares his or her school work pages with you, don't forget to take a moment to share how proud you are but at the same time hint that you feel he or she could be doing more difficult work.

10. When you meet with your child's teacher at the parent-teacher conferences, explain your theory of how all children should be taught to read. Don't allow the teacher to focus on your child's progress in reading as you know for a fact that s/he is no different than your sister-in law's child in Miss Carlisle's other 3rd grade.

11. Finally, a warning: if you have concerns about your child's progress in reading or generally in school, don't ever bring it to the attention of the school principal as s/he will discuss it with the teacher who more likely than not will take it out on your child. This of course will affect your child's entire school career, unless you plan in the near future to move to another school district where you've heard all of the children are reading above grade level and testing in the 98th percentile.

Expanding Choices
and Alternatives
for Children

By enveloping youngsters with trust and by giving them more choices as they are able to handle them, children develop greater independence, responsibility, and control over their future pathways. This is true both at home and in school.

Whenever a child or an adult makes a choice, he or she likely makes a commitment to it. This is an unwritten social convention we learn early in life. Whether it be an article of clothing a 4 year old selects from those set out by a parent the night before, a book selected from the library, a partner one chooses for a high school theater class "dialogue", or a job offer accepted following an intense interview, one sticks with the choice unless there is a very good reason to change course.

Inquiry groups

During my first year as a principal, 1968-1969, our 4th and 5th grade teachers began addressing concerns they and I had regarding the attitudes of the children towards learning. Too many of the students exhibited a limited curiosity and enthusiasm for learning, especially in the content areas. Many of the children defined learning as something the teacher did for them, not something one did for oneself. It seemed that the Sesame Street Syndrome was taking its toll: children were sitting back and waiting to be "entertained" by short, fast, exciting classroom presentations.

The staff discussed various alternatives to engage the students in taking a more active role in learning. The outgrowth of the staff brainstorming was the establishment of "Inquiry Groups" to be held one hour a week for two, four or eight week sessions. The 200 children selected a mini-course from 15-20 choices; the courses were staffed by the eight classroom teachers, the principal, other members of our staff and resource persons from the community. Courses included writing and distributing a school magazine (pre-computer, purple smudgy ditto days), creative dramatics, hand-built pottery with a local volunteer professional potter, designing, building and experimenting with model airplanes and flight, native Indian weaving and folklore with a local weaver, introduction to chess, and additional subjects based on the interests and expertise of the teachers and volunteers.

Most teachers and students reacted favorably to our first experience with a learning situation that stressed interest grouping and expanded student choice. These inquiry groups were held in the spring of 1969 and again during the 1969-1970 school year. However, we were unable to continue them the following year as the planning time, resources and energy necessary to do the program justice were not available.

Nevertheless, our experience with "inquiry groups" gave us valuable insights into how kids learn. A number of teachers tried to apply these new insights to their classroom organization and instruction in the years that followed:

- When children make a commitment to a learning activity or a goal, they become more self motivated learners.
- When children have a degree of choice in the selection of learning activities, they assume more responsibility for pursuing them in greater depth.
- When children become actively involved in their learning, they use their time more productively and with greater pride. Since the teacher is less involved "managing" the classroom, s/he is freer to focus on helping individual children learn.

The integrated day: an open unit within our school,

75 2nd–4th graders, 1971-1972

In the early 1970s, two staff members, Helen and Sue, were greatly interested in incorporating "the Integrated Day" into their classrooms, and I was very interested in learning more. Together we read and discussed this approach and its implications for our children, attended workshops, did course work at University of Connecticut, and visited schools throughout New England and New York State. This approach became known in the U.S. as

"open education" or the "informal classroom." In cooperation with Professor Vincent Rogers at U-Conn we
planned a program, for the following year, which generated its share of controversy and anxiety. (A copy of the
Open Unit Question and Answer Booklet for Parents is
included in Appendix I.)

We organized a unit of three classes, 2nd to 4th grade,
with four teachers (two experienced, two interns) which
we named the Open Unit. We selected children who we
thought could benefit from this approach, which relies
less on direct teacher motivation and more on the learning environment to stimulate the student. We then
invited parents to an orientation meeting during which
we explained the plan. Parents were given the option of
enrolling their children in the program or not. The vast
majority did, some reluctantly. As with all new programs,
some problems were encountered, and during the first
two months a few children left the program and were
transferred to "regular" classrooms.

An evaluation of the Open Unit, requested by the Board
of Education, was carried out by reviewing the scores of
the yearly administered Iowa Test of Basic Skills for the
individual children in the program, and by a comprehensive survey of the parents. The individual children's test
scores in reading compared favorably to their reading test
scores the previous year in the "regular" classrooms and
the parent surveys indicated a higher level of motivation
and self-direction on the part of most children compared
to the previous school year. (One family that was moving to a house just outside our school area in the same

town requested that their daughter, "who was doing marvelously well," be allowed to remain in the Open Unit the following year. Their request was approved by the Superintendent of Schools.)

The following is a sample of verbatim responses to a comprehensive (eight page) Parent Questionnaire completed by the Open Unit parents in March 1972. They were included as part of the program evaluation reported to the Board of Education, in which the parents were asked, "In what ways do you think we have been most successful this year?" The following responses were quite typical:

- Your success lies in the happy achievements of your students (of course I can only speak for mine). She has become more poised and more secure in her school situation. School is a part of her this year rather than her being just a small part of her school. Her curiosity has grown to encompass a vast number of subjects. She has become a more understanding person. She is learning that to compromise is not always a sign of weakness.

- We think that he has had exposure to "learning can be fun" which is exciting and interesting, and doesn't end when the bell rings.

- Awareness on my son's part that all children have strong points as well as weak points and everyone is capable of making some contribution to society.

- The school program seems to arouse a real interest in school and beyond. School doesn't end at 3:00. She seems to have more interests in more things and wants to know more about each field of interest.

- Judging from observations of my son's activities at home, I would say you have been very successful in developing a casual interest or hobby (of the student) into a more formalized study. His rock "collection" has advanced from a bag of attractive stones to a neatly arranged showcase of "gems"—- each identified by common name, place most commonly found, specific characteristics, etc. His natural love for wildlife has been directed toward more positive action—instead of merely finding the birds, he now identifies each newcomer and attempts to learn more about its diet, nesting habits, etc.

- In spite of the fact that one could scarcely ask for more in the way of intellectual progress, the outstanding success of the year for our child has been personal. We are more than pleased at the growth of self-respect which seems for our child to be the factor which enables him to confidently and actively pursue his ideas and interests. We are happy and thankful for the skill and sensitivity with which the Open Unit teachers are able to reveal the richness of the creative and intellectual possibilities of the world without imposing them upon children—to stimulate without usurping the process of discovery.

When parents were asked about their questions or concerns about the program, the breakdown was as follows:

Number of Parents	Nature of Question or Concern
39	None
7	Achievement of children in Open Unit as compared to children in the regular classroom
5	Continuity or functioning in the next grade
4	Teacher's awareness of the strengths and weaknesses of each child
4	Children avoiding certain areas of the curriculum—balanced subject exposure
3	Need for a quiet place
2	Availability of teachers for individual help
2	Evaluation of the Open Unit
2	Child not working to his fullest capacity
2	Will child learn to do unpleasant tasks?
2	Emphasis on completing work begun
1	Math instruction
1	Effect of freedom on child's behavior

1	Ability of child to plan his day
1	Marking system

When parents were asked how they would respond to their child being placed in the Open Unit the following school year (1972-73), these responses were given:

Favorable	83%
Uncertain	9%
Unfavorable	4%
No Information	4%

The integrated day:

1972-1973

Based upon our self evaluation as teachers and principal as well as parent input culled from the formal evaluation and numerous informal conversations, we modified the Open Unit the following year into two smaller units; both parents and teachers found the logistics of four teachers and 80 children too cumbersome.

While a number of parents in the school were becoming anxious that it would become one vast open education unit, the facts were that the school was becoming more pluralistic and there were more options for children. I continued to be strongly committed to supporting teachers and encouraging them to strengthen their individual teaching styles, as long as the basic guideline of respect for each child as a learner and as a person was met. Independence Elementary School had become a school where both children and teachers were valued as individuals.

Each year thereafter, when placing children in classrooms in the spring for the following year, the teachers and I tried to be very sensitive to place children with teachers and classroom structures that we felt would be most fitting and comfortable for them. We weren't always able to make a match; however, in general, I believe we were quite successful in expanding alternative classroom settings and teaching styles to motivate children.

TIME OUT FOR TRIBUTES

Patsy Smith and the Rock and Roller

Paul was an accomplished rock and roller at the age of six months. He rocked his crib back and forth with such force that he was able to rock it right out of his nursery into the hallway, past his parents' bedroom door, stopped only by the closed folding gate at the top of the stairs of the Gordons' two story home.

Paul's reputation preceded him to kindergarten. Neighborhood parents said he played too hard (a polite way of saying that he hurt their kids, broke a tooth, bruised a leg, bit a cheek). If an unsuspecting or sympathetic mother let him inside the house to play, he would certainly never be invited back. Paul would be all over the furniture or inadvertently break something in his path—a bull in a china shop.

Big and awkward for his age, obviously quite intelligent, he entered nursery school at age four, with no playmates or friends. He was a loner with a jet-propelled body. He had already been asked to leave two local private nursery schools when his parents decided to give up and keep him home until kindergarten. They were physically and emotionally frazzled by Paul. He was a four-year-old nursery school failure with a very bleak future.

Enter Patsy Smith

Patsy Smith was our Learning Disabilities Resource Room (Learning Center) teacher. She loved kids and she loved a challenge. When she heard that our kindergarten teachers and parents were beginning to panic about the prospects of Paul entering school, she came to me. "Mr. L.," she said, "Something has to be done to help these teachers and this child. Don't you agree? His reputation as a school menace is reaching fantastic proportions. It's just unbelievable what this kid is already up against."

I agreed, but couldn't imagine calling two parents into my office before the child had even entered school. What was I going to do? Tell them we've heard neighborhood rumors about their son?

"Patsy," I said, "I don't want to stir up a hornets' nest, especially in June, when teachers and parents are already tense."

I did what was least threatening to me at the time—I deferred dealing with the problem! Patsy convinced me to let her consult with the teacher from the first day of school on an unofficial basis, because she could not be legally involved with a child until he had been first fully evaluated by the appropriate professionals and officially enrolled as a special education student by the school district.

By the third week of school, Paul was in peak form and Phyllis, our gentle but firm kindergarten teacher, had given it her best. I set up a parent conference. The Gordons were so grateful that we had called them in. Finally someone was suggesting some possible routes for help. (And I had thought that I'd stir up a hornets' nest! When would I learn that tackling a problem head-on was always most effective—though at times very unpleasant?)

Paul's parents agreed to consult privately with a child psychiatrist who would explore the medical and psychological issues that might be involved in Paul's problem. His parents were unwilling to wait the month, or two, or three, or more, it would take for our psychological services to get involved. They were wise. They left my office, mother in tears of relief, father in business suit, pumping my hand endlessly in gratitude.

"When parents are so open and eager to help their child, the child can only improve," Patsy would repeat again and again. "Special education students can use every advocate they can get!"

Within a month, a meeting was held with the child psychiatrist who had recommended that a pediatric neurologist evaluate Paul. Diagnosed as an extremely hyperactive child with specific learning disabilities, Paul was placed on a blind trial of chemical therapy. The teacher kept daily records of his behavior, neither of us know-ing which days he was on the medication and which on the placebo. I reported the observations each Friday to the doctor. His hyperactivity decreased markedly when he was on the medication; after a month he was taking it on a regular basis.

Paul was now officially enrolled as a special education student and Patsy's work was cut out for her. He was identified as a child in the superior range of intelligence with significant deficits in visual memory (which makes learning to read and spell a difficult and tedious process), fine motor coordination (which affects the physical act of writing), and gross motor coordination (which affects participation in sports and free play in general).

First Patsy worked with Paul's kindergarten teacher. As his hyperactivity had markedly decreased, Paul was more receptive to the efforts of his teacher. Each bit of progress was a milestone. He could sit longer in a circle, and before long he could listen to a story through to the end. He finished a painting at the easel without waving his brush in the air to splatter paint all over the wall a-la Jackson Pollock. By December, Paul was comfortable with school routine and benefiting from most classroom activities that didn't involve the little pigeon tracks we call letters and numbers.

Patsy came to me in December. "Mr. L.," she said, "I know that it's against school district policy for LD teach-ers to work directly with children before 1st grade. Please let me work with Paul during my half-hour lunch break. He desperately needs readiness work with identifying numbers and letters. No one need know except you and me."

I couldn't disagree. I believed in early intervention, didn't I?

While Patsy possessed great power and drive, she could patiently work with a child through tedious materials and discover techniques to reach and help that child. Walking past her classroom during the noon hour, I would see her sitting nibbling on her salad while working with Paul, who was writing with thick chalk on the blackboard.

Patsy worked with Paul daily for 45 minutes or so in a small group from 1st through 4th grades in the resource room which we had, by then, renamed THE LEARNING CENTER. He first attained a solid level in reading, then in handwriting and composition. His spelling, being rather phonetic, was not particularly standard, but one knew what he was trying to say. We had always said that Paul would need a personal secretary, but technology being what it is, Paul can now use a computer and a spell-check program.

By 5th grade, Paul was in the regular classroom full time and Patsy would check in with him and his teacher from time to time, to help him deal with minor problems that arose.

Exit Patsy Smith

Patsy Smith did not have the thrill of seeing Paul graduate from high school or enter a small New England college where he majored in special education. Patsy was killed in an automobile accident when he was in 8th grade. She was 42 years old.

When Paul graduated from college he got a job as a special education teacher in a neighboring town. When he stopped by to share his wonderful news he asked if he could plant a flowering tree in the front yard of the school in Mrs. Smith's honor and memory.

He stopped by from time to time presumably to chat with me, but I knew he was checking on Mrs. Smith's tree—to make sure it was healthy and tended. He placed a small plaque at the base of the tree:

In Memory of Mrs. Patsy Smith
Thanks to a kind, caring lady who gave us kids a future.

One June he stopped by to tell me some of his success stories in class. I dug into my files and pulled out a faded 1976 purple ditto written by Patsy. I gave it to him. He had it framed to hang behind his teachers' desk.

A STATEMENT BY A SPECIAL EDUCATION TEACHER TO THE BOARD OF EDUCATION TO MAINTAIN THE SPECIAL ED BUDGET

… I must end with a short emotional plea to you from me!
- … WHEN you have experienced the change in a HYPERACTIVE pupil to one who is on task in a regular classroom

- ... WHEN you have experienced the change in a "NON-READER" who cannot recognize the 26 configurations of our alphabet to a child reading at, or near, grade level
- ... WHEN you have experienced the change in a student not able to do MATH papers because all of his numbers are reversed and inverted to a student functioning successfully at math grade level
- ... WHEN you have experienced the change in a student NOT MOTIVATED in any academic setting to the best student-tutor in the school
- ... WHEN you have experienced the change in a CLUMSY child receiving cruel jibes from classmates on the playground to the kid chosen well before last during team choose-ups
- ... WHEN you have experienced the change in a CREATIVE child whose written stories are not decipherable due to SPELLING errors to the child receiving As and Bs on all compositions
- ... WHEN you have experienced the change in an ANGRY, VIOLENT child to a cooperative active child
- ... WHEN you have experienced the change in a pupil with the inability to sort and sift out the important environmental messages from the trivial to the pupil able to quickly grasp the abstractions of a teacher presentation
- ... WHEN you have experienced the change in a student who is withdrawn in group settings to a student who readily volunteers in a regular classroom

- … WHEN you have experienced the change in a potential school dropout to a young person graduating with school personnel applauding

- … THEN, and only then, have you shared in the joy and challenge of the parent and professional involved with Special Education Students!!!!!

Patricia S. Luther
March 11th, 1976

NOTE:

There are many Patsy Smiths in our schools. This piece was written to honor our Patsy Smith (Patricia S. Luther) and all those other special education and regular classroom teachers who help the Paul Gordons and their families. (Paul is a construct of three of Patsy's pupils during her ten years at our school prior to her tragic death.)

Not every special education student is a glowing success, but many are and for every success there is a Patsy Smith working in concert with skilled, caring and dedicated classroom teachers, alongside supportive and appreciative parents.

Not a month goes by that I don't think of Patsy and all I learned from her.

A Portrait of Cecil Kittle

Shared in the Friday school newsletter in honor of his 10th year at our school (November, 1978)

Next week Mr. Kittle undergoes ear surgery to hopefully regain the hearing he has been losing over the past twenty years. We will surely miss all of the "Hi, Mr. Kittles" until he returns to school shortly after New Year's Day.

"Hi, Mr. Kittle" is music to my ears. I recall when Sammy, a 2nd grader, greeted me with a "Hi, Mr. Kittle" when I entered his classroom last spring. Sammy certainly knew I wasn't Mr. Kittle. In his own way, Sammy was telling me that he had come a long way in a year. The previous year I had reprimanded him a number of times for disturbing his class and fighting on the playground. But this past year he was making wonderful progress in learning how to play with other children. That day, I was his friend, Mr. Kittle.

Mr. Kittle is our head custodian. His helpfulness and friendliness is not listed in any Board of Education job description. He will help anyone he meets. Throughout the school day he can be observed welcoming a newcomer into the building, helping a group of children plant a garden in the school courtyard, discussing an infraction of a school rule in a friendly manner with a child, reassuring a younger child who has dropped her lunch tray in the hallway that she needn't cry, or any of a host of other friendly gestures. Many an evening he attends Little League or soccer games on various playgrounds in town, and cheers on our students who may even be on opposing teams.

He takes great pride in his school—his children, his teachers, his building. He sets a very influential example. Although always busy, he always has time to listen and to be your friend. He's not only a friend, but the "uncle" or "grandfather" that a child may never have known or who may live too far away to be an empathetic listener.

Both Sammy and I had a good feeling deep down inside when he called me his friend Mr. Kittle that day.

Helen

A tribute in memory of a fellow teacher and beloved friend

JUDITH W. GARDNER
(September 2, 1993)

A memorial service is a glance back at the past. But we are all involved today in looking forward to the new school year, and that is much more fitting to Helen. She never liked good-byes. A true teacher, she was focused on possibilities and, although avidly interested in history, she was always ready for the new. Speaking of Helen in this school courtyard at the opening of the school year is most appropriate, because her very life was an affirmation of our work, which we begin anew today. Her life, like ours, was devoted to the future.

When we think about Helen, we think about teaching. As so often happens in our profession, much of what I learned from Helen came not from things she told me (although she told me much), but from who she was. She gave me a new way of listening, because of the person she was. I remember sitting in faculty meetings, when I was a new teacher, and hearing Helen say something that took me by surprise, that did not match my own thinking at all. I'd dismiss it as somewhat tangential, go back to work, and find weeks later that the truth of her remark was borne out in the events of the classroom. Gradually, I learned to file away those comments that were not immediately clear to me, to trust that they came from a perspective different from, but as valuable and often more insightful than my own. I learned to listen with patience and faith; and my students today, when they are heard with a more patient and faithful ear, are recipients of Helen's legacy.

A principal, setting out to evaluate Helen, instead received a lesson about teaching, by observing her. He walked into the classroom, saw that she was not present-ing a lesson, and decided to return at another time. The next time he entered the classroom, he again could see no lesson being delivered. The third time, he realized he'd better stay. He listened and he watched. And being a wise man, he became a student in Helen's classroom that day.

What he saw was a teacher who fit the description from the Taoist Lao Zi, who said this about rulers:

> The best of all rulers is but a shadowy presence to his subjects …
> When his task is accomplished and his work done/The people all say, "It happened to us naturally."

But of course intense concentration lay behind her accomplishments. She not only kept abreast of current thought about learning; she immersed herself in bringing to a practical, useful stage what to most of us is just the-ory. When learning theory began to address the different functions of the two sides of the brain, Helen entered into a five-year experiment, to change her own way of thinking from the traditional to the more creative. She forced herself to think differently, in an attempt to develop within herself what was being described as right-brain abilities, as a means of gaining true, experiential understanding of a potentially powerful means of helping children learn.

In recent years, Helen was interested in the ways in which modern culture, as it shifted from print media to television and electronics, was reshaping our children as learners. Not one to harness the human mind to a single way of functioning, Helen believed that if something wasn't working in the "student + curriculum = learning" equation, the part of the equation that could never be wrong was the student. She believed it is our job as teachers to find a way to present curriculum that fits the student's way of perceiving. I urged her to define and describe these changes in the ways children learn, to help us understand and better serve today's students. I knew she possessed both depth of knowledge and the carefully developed ability to make a creative leap to take us to new ground. But she would not leave the classroom for the study of educational issues. Her classroom was her laboratory. She would not take her finger from its pulse. The difference she could make in one child's life meant more to her than publications or the recognition that might come from them.

Helen studied her students. Knowing that surmounting difficulties engenders confidence, she was persistent in finding ways to help her students overcome weakness.

But it was the very best within each child that captivated her. She searched for it, she located it, and that is what she nourished. She knew that therein lay the hope for her children, and she dedicated her life to finding, shaping, and encouraging the "best" within them. Even immobile on her hospital bed, she was still directing me to make contacts that could lead to opportunities for a former student, who had come back to tell her his dreams.

I thought about the life of a teacher, while gazing upon an ancient tablet in China, as my friend lay dying. The words had been "carved in stone," to last for ages. However, time had erased these words, as time will; and permanence eluded the carver. I thought about permanence, about significance, about the work we teachers do each day. It is not seen, as plainly as that message had been seen, by millions of eyes over hundreds of years. But our etching runs deep and has significance and perhaps a permanence beyond the lives we directly touch. Helen's work has changed the children she taught. They in turn will bring something more of their gifts to those whose lives they will touch. By sharing her insights, her understanding, her love of teaching with us, Helen has changed me and some of you. And her work will touch our students and those whose lives they affect in turn.

I've talked about Helen the teacher, but she was a many-faceted woman. Our friendship grew out of respect and deepened into a trust that never failed us. As her friend, I have felt the sharp pain of missing her and the soft-edged sadness of that loss. But always there is the joy of a deep friendship that remains, the continual blessing of having known her. And for us all, as we go to our busy class-rooms, our "overwhelming" job, as she always said it was, we can take with us her sense of reverence for what we do, the legacy of one who was a teacher among us, to those of us who still carry on her precious work.

TESTING

Get your facts first and then you can distort them as much as you wish.

Mark Twain

Say you were standing with one foot in the oven and one foot in an ice bucket. According to the percentage people, you should be perfectly comfortable.

Bobby Bragan

I abhor averages. I like the individual case. A man may have six meals one day and none the next, making an average of three meals per day, but that is not a good way to live.

Louis D. Brandeis

Testing Absurdities

Independence Public Schools
Independence, Connecticut

To: 1st grade Teachers
From: Miss Kathleen Winston
Director of Guidance and Testing
Date: November 21, 1963
Re: Kuhlman-Anderson Intelligence Testing

This test will not be an easy one to give. It is not that the directions are so complicated, but rather that every item on the test is finely timed. Unfortunately there are no stop watches available for the classroom teachers. It is suggested that you use an alternative method for timing as follows: count to yourself, one-ten thousandths, two-ten thousandths, three-ten thousandths, and so on. If these words are said at a fairly quick but even and comfortable pace, the amount of time elapsed between one and two will be one second. Perhaps you have a sweep hand on some clock whereby you could test yourself before you give the test.

Suggestions for administering ...
Good luck!

Author's reaction:

I found this "one ten-thousandths, two ten-thousandths" memo while weeding out files accumulated by former principals. I could not believe that the school district had previously been administering standardized group intelligence testing to 1st graders. I had a mental picture of first grade teachers metamorphosed into human stop watches as their anxious six year olds were apprehensively marking hand-scoreable record booklets.

The Kuhlmann-Anderson (Frederick and Rose) test, developed in the 1920s, was a 50 minute group test with mostly non-verbal test items in the early grades. The "experts" claimed that the Kuhlmann-Anderson correlated well with school performance and other intelligence tests. I maintain that Frederick's and Rose's test, along with other such group intelligence tests (Slosson, Otis-Lennon, etc.), do nothing more than categorize, classify and pigeonhole youngsters who are too young to protect themselves from the limits imposed upon them by mostly well meaning adults—adults who place more faith in mass testing than in their own observations and judgments. In fact, very little has changed since 1927 when Rose and Frederick copyrighted their test which hundreds of millions of test detesters have endured during the past four generations.

The testing mania in today's schools generated by the NO CHILD LEFT BEHIND federal legislation has led to new levels of distrusting teacher judgment, draining of teachers' creative energies and robbing children of hours during which they could be actively and passionately engaged in constructive educational pursuits.

Teacher Work Day

August 31, 1977
5:30 p.m.

Dear Mr. L,

The custodians have left for the evening and we sit here alone feeling outraged by this morning's meeting. After listening to the Superintendent, principals, and curriculum directors for nearly three hours during the elementary staff meeting, we wonder what we are doing here. We have been together on the staff for more than five years, and each year there is a little more pressure from the central administration (sometimes subtle, often not) to put more emphasis on this or that, to improve the results of standardized test scores, or to prove that what we are doing is in fact paying off.

At 9:00 this morning we were eager to meet colleagues we hadn't seen all summer and to prepare for the opening of school and our first day with our new students. By 12:00 noon, none of us wanted to step into the building ever again. It seems that the central administration wants pre-and post-tests in just about every subject area, to prove to the Board of Education and to the public what a great job we are doing, or to identify those areas where we are not meeting their standards. It seems that anything below the 90th percentile is a problem to the administration.

The only positive comment made today at the meeting—besides how important teachers are to the educational process (really now)—was regarding the 3rd grade's spelling. It seems that the 3rd grade spelling is in "good shape" and that the primary teachers should continue doing whatever we are doing right to get test results in the 98th percentile. We guess that if we spent half of each day drilling children in punctuation and usage we might be able to bring that up to the 98th percentile. What a pity that our children only scored in the 89th percentile! We suppose that since we shall be expected to do so much testing this year teaching will be of secondary importance.

We almost died when the time inventory was passed out and the 1,776 minutes per week were divided up into neat packages—200 minutes for math, 425 for reading, 40 for music, 40 for art, etc. No time was allocated for helping children grow as human beings. Since the administration has not come up with a pre-and post-test for caring or sharing or consideration, should we assume that we should not waste any of the valuable 1,776 minutes on those non-curriculum concerns? Shall we ignore the child who comes into school upset because of a family argument or a bus problem with another child? What about the child who brings in something special to share from his trip to the rock quarry? Will we have time to acknowledge his enthusiasm? We certainly won't have time to extend a budding interest in geology; that isn't in the curriculum until 4th grade.

We will be here on opening day. We will comply with all of the directives pronounced at this morning's meeting. Maybe our test results will even improve. If we can't be trusted by the central administration to make judgments about individual student progress or to try out a new approach or material with a child that might succeed beyond our wildest expectations or fail miserably, we certainly can't hope to serve as model learners to our students. Model robots, maybe.

If you still trust us to inspire our children and to teach them as individuals who may not all reach the 98th percentile, please smile when you meet us in the hallways on opening day and visit our classes often, very often. We need your encouragement!

Here's hoping,

Sharon, Pat and Judy
(The 2nd grade Team)

NOTE:

This piece tries to convey the concerns and sentiments teachers shared with me during the early years of the accountability movement. I believe it resonates even more loudly today as the testing movement has become firmly entrenched at the state level and embedded in the heart of the 2002 No Child Left Behind (NCLB) federal legislation which deifies the TEST as King of the Mountain.[2]

The phrase, "the tyranny of testing," coined by Banesh Hoffman for his classic 1962 critique of certain aspects of testing[3], is a fitting description of the testing quagmire into which American education now finds itself slowly sinking deeper and deeper.

INDEPENDENCE PUBLIC SCHOOLS

INDEPENDENCE, CONNECTICUT

June 15, 2006

Announcement of Vacancy

Position: Director of Elementary Teacher/Test Preparation Specialists
> (formerly Director of Elementary Education)

Salary Range: $118,000-$143,000 (12 month position)

Qualifications:

- *Ph.D. in the field of Measurement, Evaluation and Assessment* (MEA)
- Thorough working knowledge of state and federal educational regulations and of the field of assessment and targeted instruction to meet minimum educational competencies of state and NCLB standards.
- Strong collaborative and interpersonal skills to lead teachers, parents, and members of the school and

of the greater community to understand and support a *test centered* elementary school curriculum.

Job Description:

- Supervise recruitment and hiring of an elementary staff committed to and well trained in a focused *test centered* educational program of studies.
- Responsible for supervision and evaluation of Elementary Teacher/Test Preparation Specialists.
- Responsible for intensive staff in-service training with the following goals:

    a) to improve test taking skills of students in grades K-6, including outreach to local nursery schools, early childhood and daycare centers

    b) to provide training to the elementary teacher/ test preparation specialists to insure that the individual test scores of all students in the areas of reading and math meet a minimal level of achievement prior to the year 2014 as mandated in the No Child Left Behind Act.

- Allocate appropriate resources and time during the elementary school day and week to insure that the average percentiles in reading and math in the Independence Public Schools will rank among the top 3 school districts in the state of Connecticut by 2009.

- Act as liaison with the local Realty Board of Directors to corroborate yearly the positive correlation between the rise in the school district's annual test profile with the cost of homes purchased in the town of Independence during the same time period. If the correlation is a negative one, the Director is to determine which actions should be taken by the total elementary staff to insure that this upward trend is reestablished.
- Liaison with the school psychological department, individual school nurses and local pediatricians and psychologists to identify and counsel the increasing number of students who display "test anxiety syndrome" symptoms and higher levels of class and school absenteeism.
- Liaison with school principals to identify and counsel staff members who are experiencing high levels of absenteeism and "burn out" as well as manifesting dysfunctional teaching behaviors resulting from the school district's shift from a child centered school culture to a *test centered* school culture.

cc: Chairperson, Independence Board of Education
President, Independence Teachers Association
Chairperson, Independence Realty Board of Directors
Director, Independence Child and Family Services
The Wizard of Oz, Emerald City

THE INS AND OUTS OF THE SCHOOL OFFICE

The First Day

I hadn't noticed the grey Chevrolet parked outside my office window. It was the first day of my second year as principal and I thought I had been thoroughly prepared for the arrival of the children. Their 510 sparkling, scrubbed faces hid their apprehension as they passed through the freshly painted front door. I stood in the school lobby greeting each child.

I, too, was anxious: Please let the first day run smoothly. All of the details had been attended to—schedules prepared, teachers briefed, bus lists cross-checked, meetings held, textbooks distributed.... My secretary and I had even remembered to reset the master clock. Imagine the confusion the teachers would have felt if the bells had rung at the wrong hours. If the end of recess bell failed to ring, this would be the happiest first day in the history of American education.

Teachers were greeting the youngsters in the hallway and helping those few lost souls looking particularly confused, distressed, or on the verge of tears. By 9:00, 509 children had found their way to their classrooms. The children disappeared from the hallways, classroom doors swung closed. The silence in the school was eerie.

The children, on their best behavior (reserved for company at home or the first day of school) sat quietly waiting for their teacher to speak. Attendance would be taken, classroom rules reviewed and then everyone, teachers and children alike, would breathe a sigh of relief. This was the moment of judgment, when kids told themselves that this year would be great, or not so bad, or one that they'd just sit out.

The teachers could forget their annual night-before nightmares. They dared to relax a bit. They were satisfied that the children actually listened to them and were not wildly protesting against the classroom rules. The teachers were in charge and there hadn't been a mini French Revolution.

As the atmosphere in the classrooms was becoming more relaxed, my secretary and I sat down to enjoy our first leisurely cup of coffee in a week. Congratulations were in order as everything was going smoothly. All that remained today was to see that 510 children were fed and that each one boarded the right bus home at 3:15. Hopefully the transportation department wouldn't call at

4:00, with one bewildered child still on the bus at the end of the run.

We looked at each other and laughed nervously, not knowing what to do next. We continued to sip our coffee and to marvel at how quiet the school was. These moments of complete relaxation were abruptly interrupted by the arrival of a very sweet but frantic woman in the reception area. Her son, Scott, was sitting outside in her car and refusing to come in. His friends had told him that his second grade teacher was the school witch. Scott had spent the greater part of the summer being a nervous wreck.

I went outside with Scott's mom, confident that using my influence, I would convince him to come in. I would explain that his teacher was a nice lady (which she was) and that he had no reason to worry. His response was unexpected: he looked up at me, covered his ears with both hands, and wouldn't budge an inch from the back seat. Well, my approach obviously wasn't going to work. I certainly was not going to use physical force to pull him out and drag him screaming into the building. I believed in reason, kindness, and child psychology, didn't I?

Stalling for time to think, I suggested to his mom that we return to the building and talk over a cup of coffee (my third cup since breakfast and it was still only 9:20!). Did I feel stupid? A second year principal—the "authority figure" in the school—not being able to convince a seven-year-old to come into school!

Once inside, she calmed down a bit. Scott's mother (whom I shall call Ms. Dee) explained that he had always been a shy, sensitive child. This, compounded by a whole summer of worrying about his new teacher, had upset her too. Her tears then began to flow, and Ms. Dee lost control of herself. Here I was with an almost complete stranger crying her heart out and all I could do was hand her a box of tissues.

I tried to comfort her, but did so in a most awkward fashion. Nothing I said seemed to help—it only made things worse. So I just sat there, embarrassed for the poor woman, waiting for her to calm down and pull herself together. I certainly had a lot to learn about dealing with hysterical people.

We sat for another ten or fifteen minutes as Ms. Dee regained a state of semi-composure. We were hoping that Scott would tire of sitting in the car and would emerge on his own volition. No such luck!

As my secretary poured mom more coffee, we peered out of my office window as nonchalantly as possible to check on Scott. He was sitting there rigidly and definitely did not intend to budge. In fact, he looked as if he were preparing himself for a prolonged sit-in or hunger strike (remember, this was the 1960s).

Here we were, two apparently competent adults in our thirties, unable to convince a seven-year-old to open the car door, walk twenty steps to the front door and another fifty to his classroom. What I needed now was Glenda the Good Witch and some magic shoes for Scott.

I began to semi-panic. I was familiar with the literature on school phobia and the reluctance of some mothers to separate from their youngsters, but was I, a novice

principal, prepared to run a school? My panic was interrupted by the strident ringing of the intercom. Scott's
second grade teacher was looking for her missing student. Another child, who had gotten a ride to school with
Scott's mother, casually mentioned to the teacher about
half an hour after school began that she thought Scott
was supposed to be in her class.

Not wishing to explain to 27 second graders with ears
glued to the intercom that Scott was staging a sit-in in his
car, I went down to the classroom to speak privately with
the teacher. She suggested that she give it a try, and went
outside to speak with him. She returned a few minutes
later, frustrated that not only had she failed, but he had
by then locked all of the car doors.

Although I hadn't the slightest idea of what to do at
this point, I knew for certain that his mother shouldn't
drive him home, as it would be even more difficult to get
him to school the next day.

Scott's mother and I made small-talk for another few
minutes, hoping time would be on our side. I was envis-
aging the two of us sitting in my office all morning, when
a possible strategy occurred to me. If Scott's mom were
driven home in another car, there would be one person
fewer involved in this dilemma. And if this were a power
struggle between mother and child, one fewer player
would be on the scene. Scott's mom was reluctant to leave
at first, but realized she could do nothing to help. Trying
to contain her embarrassment, she telephoned a neighbor
to pick her up. I cringed, picturing myself in her shoes,
but thought this might be the best course of action.

As his mother got into her neighbor's car and slowly drove out of the parking lot, we had one surprised little boy jumping out of the car to see what his mom was doing. At the same time, our custodian, Mr. Kittle, was observing the whole scene as he swept the front sidewalk. When Scott began to run after the car, Mr. Kittle dropped his broom, ran to Scott, and gently placed his hand on his shoulder. He then calmly walked him into the building and into the classroom, chatting about the summer holidays, the town pool, and Little League.

Scott got through the first day and year without further incident. His mom stopped by my office a few years later to tell me that at the time of the problem, her marriage was breaking up and she thought that Scott's unforgettable performance on his first day of 2nd grade might have been related to all of the goings-on at home. She apologized unnecessarily.

Mr. Kittle, who got me through this first day, stayed on as custodian for the next twenty years. He was always ready to stop and listen—a good friend to kids, teachers, parents, and principal alike. He was our resident granddad!

Every school and institution, if it is to be humane, needs heart centers. One of ours glowed in the darkness of the dimly-lit custodian's "office" wedged between the kitchen and the furnace room.

A Taiwanese Student Visits Our School

We arrive at Independence Alimentary School at five after ten. The principal stood in the front entryway to greet us. Having dark hair, mild eyes, mustache, and an intimate round abdomen, the young principal took us to his office and told us our morning schedule.

My whole feeling to this school is "pleasant," especially to those adorable students. They are students from kindergarten to the 5th grade, and truly they are the heart of the school. That is such a wonderful feeling to see that they are still keeping their curious, open, and fresh minds, which seem to gradually disappear among American children in their rapidly moving society.

It was a sweet experience; I will never forget these lovely, lucky children.

Ya-Pei Huang
University Student
Visiting from Taiwan
May 1981

NOTE:

The university teacher who brought a small group of students to visit schools in our town sent me a copy of this student's observations shortly after her visit. I shall never forget my "intimate round abdomen" nor her other unpre-

120

tentious remarks. I have saved her note amongst my collection of school memories for the past 24 years!

Saved by My
Secretary!

How do you muster the courage to telephone a mother to explain that her 2nd grade son is spraying the girls on the playground at recess time with her contraceptive foam?

You don't! The cowardly side of you wins out, and sheepishly you ask your secretary to make the call for you.

Mom's good natured reply: "Well, you see, at least I'm trying."

A Minute of
Silence, Please!

When the Connecticut legislature passed the school meditation law in the 1970s, the lawmakers did not have the transcendental variety in mind. As the Supreme Court had ruled against prayer in the public schools in 1965, bringing meditation into the school was considered a workable compromise by the legislators.

So at 9:00 each morning, immediately after the last bus had arrived at our school and all of the children had entered their classrooms, the day began with, "May I have everyone's attention please," on the intercom. This was repeated twice to get the attention of the children who were busy talking with their friends before the school day officially began. Then Mrs. Woodhouse, our office receptionist, announced, "A minute of silence will now begin." If the telephone should happen to ring, possibly a mother calling to say that her child had forgotten his lunch, Mrs. Woodhouse would say, in her quietest voice: "Please hold. We're meditating."

If a parent or visitor came into the building during the minute of silence, confusion would set in as she or he looked up and down the hallway, and saw only frozen tableaux. If said person walked into the office and asked in a normal tone of voice, "What is everyone doing?"

which was amplified by the total silence, Mrs. Woodhouse would whisper "A MINUTE OF SILENCE." "Oh?" Still total bewilderment.

Most of the children had no idea why they had to stop dead in their tracks at the beginning of each school day. If a child asked a teacher why we had a minute of silence, she might have answered "it's a law" or "think some good thoughts, son." Many children thought it was a chance for the teachers to collect their thoughts before the school day began.

Even the Fire Marshal, Howard Howards, had an encounter with the minute of silence. Each October, Howard conducted a surprise fire drill during Fire Prevention Week. Actually, after he had sprung his surprise fire drill during lunch and recess for two or three consecutive Octobers, causing mass confusion, we finally convinced him to change his routine and not disrupt our school during the noon hour.

So, this past year, the first year of meditation, he began his rounds of the town's schools at our school. The surprise fire drill at 9 a.m. surprised him as well. When he pulled the fire alarm right by the front exit, he immediately dashed outside to time the evacuation of the building. His goal was to complete the evacuation in one minute or less. But no one came out!

Before too many seconds passed, he ran into the office raising his voice at his old high school classmate, Mrs. Woodhouse: "My god, my god! What's going ..." Before he could finish his sentence, Mrs. Woodhouse looked her old friend in the eye and whispered as loudly as she could, "SILENT PRAYERS, please Howard."

Howard bowed his head. At the end of the minute when all those who were in the office lifted their heads and returned to work, Howard went out of the front door to sit in his car waiting to try again. Immediately thereafter, unaware that Howard was going to set off the fire alarm a second time, I went to the intercom and asked everyone to evacuate the building, as the fire alarm takes precedence over everything else including meditation. I walked out of the office and blocked the front exit, as I often blocked an exit to prepare for the remote possibility of a smoke filled hallway. Everyone silently exited to the side and rear of the building.

Immediately after everyone had vacated the building, Howard came in the front door and tried again to ring a surprise fire drill for Fire Prevention Week. Howard was very angry when he came running back inside again because no one was vacating the building for the second fire drill in five minutes. There was no one to be found in the office or hallways. What a way to start the day, especially for a farmer who donates his services as the volunteer Fire Marshal!

In this age of constant interruptions, I must write a note of thanks to the Connecticut legislature for having given me the luxury of a daily minute of silence. I began to appreciate how long a minute actually was, and how much substance was lost by being rushed through time by impatient people and bureaucratic deadlines. Perhaps we should open the school day with half-an-hour of meditation.

Drills!

It was the early 1960s. A distinguished looking gentleman calmly walked onto the stage from the wings and interrupted the speaker, C. Eric Lincoln, who was lecturing on the Black Muslims at Boston's Ford Hall Forum. Taking the microphone, he asked for our cooperation in clearing the auditorium as quickly and as quietly as possible. Nothing more was said.

Two thousand people silently left the hall, all looking nervously into the eyes of the strangers from the oncoming aisles, all discretely sniffing for signs of smoke. Once we were outside, the police told us that a bomb threat had been received only minutes before against the life of Mr. Lincoln, an African American. How thankful I was that all of those in the hall had practiced evacuating a building a hundred or more times during their school days, thereby reducing the possibility of panic—a sure killer.

Whether it is fire drills, earthquake drills, tornado drills, or air raid drills, we've all had our fair share of drills. We, teachers and principals, have been drilled out. But for good reason.

However, in the 1970s it was difficult to fathom the State Department of Education's requirement that a set of procedures for evacuation of all children in the event of sufficient warning of an atomic attack be distributed annually to all school principals. Yearly, we principals filed away the updated atomic evacuation plan, knowing it would be futile to spend another quarter of a second on it. Furthermore, if we thought seriously about it, we'd all be crazy.

I suppose the school evacuation plan made about as much sense as the State of Connecticut plan to evacuate the entire population of each town to a paired town in Vermont or New Hampshire at a supposedly safe distance from the "urban industrial complex." (Can you imagine the traffic jam? Everything would come to a complete standstill, and we'd all die in a mass of carbon monoxide fumes while deafened and driven out of our minds by the blasts of thousands upon thousands of honking horns.)

Back to fire drills. Unlike atomic evacuation plans, I did take fire drills seriously. The first of my monthly fire drills in 1968 was a disaster. Children were pushing, darting in and out, and laughing and shouting so much so that it was impossible for an adult to give directions, such as to exit through an alternate route, in case of a real fire. Orderly it wasn't!

At the next staff meeting, everyone was very receptive to calming the children during fire drills as the teachers, too, were disturbed by the confusion and the lack of understanding of the seriousness of emergency situations. "Only walking, no talking," became the byword, and within a few months the fire drills were carried out in an orderly fashion. Only after a lost child was found bewildered in a toilet stall did we make certain that no one was left inside the school, in case of a real fire.

During one fire drill, we actually had a fire. The kitchen staff rushed out of the side kitchen door and had forgotten to shut off one oven. When the kitchen staff prematurely re-entered the building, the kitchen and adjoining hallway were filled with smoke from pizza burning to a crisp. They called the office in panic and everyone was—much to their surprise—barred from re-entering their "burning" school.

(Wasn't it one of your recurring childhood dreams that your school burned down one summer night and you had a year off while it was being rebuilt? It was one of my favorites.)

On a previous occasion, one of our 4th graders, a frequent visitor to the boys' room, was experimenting with matches (as if he didn't really know what happens when one lights a match), and dropped one into a metal waste paper receptacle filled with paper towels. Once the fire was set, he "thoughtfully" went immediately into the hallway and pulled down the red fire alarm lever. The building was evacuated calmly and quickly and the volunteer firemen appeared in what seemed like no time at all, as the firehouse was only a few hundred yards down the road. The very efficient and courteous on-duty crew of two entered the building with their axes and long fire hoses to put out the blaze in the trash can, only to find that it had already been extinguished by the custodian; Mr. Kittle had been mopping the kitchen floor across the hall, and had put the fire out with his pail of dirty water.

At this point our major problem began. We didn't know how to silence the fire alarm. Who knew that the shattered glass in the alarm box had to be replaced? Certainly I didn't (I am technically illiterate). Nor did anyone else in the school. The alarm blared for four … five … six … seven … eight minutes. The children and teachers waited patiently for the fire to be extinguished. (Of course, they saw no signs of their school burning down.) Those of us remaining in the building, the two firemen, the custodian, the secretary and I, felt as if our heads were about to implode from the horn blasts, and we hadn't a clue how to shut off the damn alarm.

Finally the volunteer fire chief arrived on the scene. He *thought* he'd left his gas station to oversee his men putting out a blaze in a burning school, but instead he had to help a bewildered principal turn off the head splitting alarm which was blasting at steady three-second intervals. The fire chief immediately dashed out of the building. A moment later, additional fire trucks arrived from Fire Station #2 across town, as the alarm continued ringing. Imagine the looks on the faces of the children and teachers—still lined up outside—when they saw more fire trucks arriving. This was it! No more school for weeks. The teachers could envision their new spring bulletin board displays going up in smoke, and the kids were certain that the books and trading cards in their desks would add fuel to the fire.

Less than five minutes later, the fire chief ran back into the building holding something in his raised hand, as if he were approaching the finishing line of the Boston Marathon. He had an almost invisible tube of glass, which he had located somewhere in the firehouse. He inserted it in the alarm box, and then—silence! We looked at each other in disbelief, so much so that we almost forgot to ring the bell to signal everyone to come back into the building.

I sensed a sigh of relief as everyone reentered the building. But there was also a definite air of let-down—that long-awaited unforeseen school holiday wasn't going to materialize.

Everything quickly returned to normal. Only the ringing in our ears lingered on into the day. The fire chief stopped in the next day with a little gift for me—two small pieces of tubular glass. I carefully placed them in an envelope, which I marked and taped to the side of my left-hand desk drawer—never to be used again, but left as my gift to the next principal.

On Cleaning Out a Principal's Desk Drawer

July 1975

Just before leaving my office for summer vacation, I performed my yearly ritual—rummaging through an array of artifacts deposited in my deep left-hand desk drawer. My 1974-1975 dig included confiscated items, unclaimed items, lost items, first-aid items, items to ponder, items for emergencies:

1 battery-operated miniature fan	(Brought in by one budding inventor and researcher ostensibly to cool himself off. Taken away when he was using it to see how close he could get to girls' faces without removing their noses!)
4 clear plastic rulers	(Never could find one when needed—always settled to the bottom like silt)
1 tattered hardball	(Unclaimed, unusable, and under no circumstances allowed—softballs only, for safety reasons)

1 piece of Bubble Yum bubble gum	(Could be used as a cement building block or as decorative Lego©)
2 atomic bomb cap igniters	(We're still in the midst of the Cold War—the onset of the Atomic Age was a mere thirty years ago)
1 old-fashioned beer can opener	(Kept in my top drawer to rescue teachers and scout leaders having parties. I'd panic too if I had 27 children waiting with empty cups and I couldn't possibly get the Hi-C drink out of its metallic container)
1 blue vinyl wallet with $1.73 in change, several unfamiliar pictures, and no name	(Has sat unclaimed for three years. With the current rampant inflation and high interest rates, I should have banked it—it would have been worth $2.00 by now)
1 book of matches in an envelope marked "Jeffrey the Firefly"	(Must make a mental note about Jeffrey as part of my personal Fire Prevention Awareness Program)

2 thin tubes of glass in a 6x9 brown envelope taped to the inside of my desk drawer and marked EMERGENCY	(To rescue the principal if a fire alarm is pulled. For further instructions how to STOP the blasted alarm, see "Drills!")
2 matchbox cars	(Thrown up in the air in the kindergarten sandbox to crash land wherever. Unclaimed, as the owner moved away after having been in our school for only three weeks, to the utter relief of the teacher—and the principal)
1 hard candy wrapped in strawberry decorated paper	(Placed gently in the palm of my hand on my very first day as principal six years earlier by Jennifer on her first day in kindergarten. Jennifer, with her long blond braids and freckled smile, carries her effervescent air everywhere. I keep her gift in my drawer to continually remind me of the sweetness and trusting nature of youngsters as they eagerly venture into the world of school life)

5 notes from parents not needing a response

Mrs. Anderson's being the most amusing this year.

Monday, January 6th

Dear Mr. Lakin,

I am cowered with embarrassment for having called you Friday night. The shoes Ralphie was so convinced he had left in school were at a neighbor's. You'd think by the time you got to your fifth child, you'd know enough not to believe him too much. At any rate, I apologize for bothering you at home and it won't happen again.

Sincerely, Katherine Anderson

I wonder what an anthropologist would conclude about our schools and times if my desk drawer were excavated 1,000 years from now!

BUREAUCRACY

A vicious cycle is launched: the more paperwork teachers are asked to do, the less time they have for teaching, the less time they have for teaching, the less learning occurs; the less learning, the more the demand for paperwork intended to ensure that teachers are teaching as the bureaucracy insists they should.[4]

Professor Linda Darling-Hammond

In a typical school, the principal manages, but she does not have the power to organize a school, and she takes few risks because risk taking is discouraged. In a centralized top-down school district ... a principal is not free to deviate from ... bureaucratic and contractual requirements.

An entrepreneur is a principal who has the freedom to organize her school in whatever way will work best for both students and staff. That is to say, the entrepreneur is a problem-solver rather than a rule follower ... It means that they (entrepreneurial principals) are focused on solving every problem that stands in the way of student achievement.[5]

Professor William G. Ouchi

Breaking Barriers

My first encounter with educational bureaucracy was at the University of Michigan the moment I naively inquired about becoming certified as an elementary school teacher in the state of Michigan. I found that I hadn't followed the prescribed educational pattern or sequence: I hadn't attended a teachers' college nor enrolled in the education department of the university. Nevertheless, I had just completed my M.A. degree in sociology and wanted to become a teacher.

I had been influenced by the sensitive and inspired work that my wife had been doing with her 6th graders in Willow Run, and by all of the teachers with whom I had come into contact while I carried out a Master's thesis project in two elementary schools in Ann Arbor. As part of a grant awarded to the Institute for Social Research I had spent two days a week for most of a semester conducting non-participant observation in a small school with mainly minority children, and in a larger, basically white, middle class, suburban school. Both schools shared the same principal. I was in awe of the humanistic and dedicated attitude of the staff, and I wanted to join them in their profession.

When the certification advisor in the university's education department advised me that as an out-of-state student I would need an additional 52 hours of course credit

to satisfy the state of Michigan's certification requirements for a temporary certificate, I couldn't believe his
words. I thought he must've been joking. He wasn't. Two
more years of university work to prepare as an elementary
teacher only because I was not from Michigan seemed
completely unreasonable. I was prepared to study for
another year, but not two. Moreover, I felt that I already
possessed many of the skills of the young, less experienced
teachers I had observed during the previous year.

Not allowing myself to be too discouraged by the
bureaucracy, I enrolled in evening education courses in
a nearby teachers college and began to substitute teach.
Needless to say, most of my learning took place during
the daytime. I welcomed the opportunity to work with
a real class and to interact with children of so many ages
and backgrounds.

Debbie, however, almost ended my educational career
before its onset. I was assigned a class of 6th graders in a
completely segregated minority school in Ypsilanti for a
full week. The teacher for whom I was substituting was
recovering from a bout of mental exhaustion from working with this class, and was into her second week of recu-
peration. I believe the substitute from the previous week
was also at home recovering.

I'm certain I learned more about the quality of race relations and educational conditions for minority children in
that one week than I have in all the years since then. With
the assistance of the African American principal, whose
advice I sought during the first morning recess, I survived
the week. I explained that I had become so angry with

the class, which was trying out every known antic to test me out, that I had sworn at the children. Much to my surprise I had blurted out, "What the hell is going on here?"—mild language to be sure considering some of the language the class was using, but I had never known a teacher to use profanity in the classroom. The fatherly principal assured me that my language was the least of the problems and he advised me to send any troublemaker to him. He decided to set an example for the class and asked me to identify the person who had caused the most trouble, and he would send that child home for the remainder of the week. As fourteen-year-old Debbie had caused the most disruption, that decision would be very easy for me to make. She was sent home and the remainder of the morning went without major problems.

When class resumed in the afternoon, our first few minutes of quiet work were interrupted by Debbie, standing outside the high windows of our basement room, jumping up and down and doing animal imitations. The class thought Debbie was uproarious. Taking a few moments to collect myself, I called the principal on the wall phone for help, not thinking beforehand to pull the blackout drapes. It was a lost day. Debbie had certainly beaten me down. I knew I couldn't let everyone go home for the day, so I tried in vain to teach.

However, the kids worked fairly well for the remainder of the week, after I had promised them that they could have a Valentine's Day party on Friday if they settled down and did a reasonable amount of work. (Many of the children were reading and doing arithmetic quite below 6th grade level.)

The class organized the party on their own and Friday finally came. Everything went along as well as could be expected for a school party until someone started to throw popcorn. I figured there was no sense in trying to interfere since it would probably only make matters worse. The worst that could happen was that we'd have a lot of sweeping up to do before we went home. I walked out of the confusion of the classroom to calm myself down for a few moments. As I waited-out the popcorn fight standing by the door in the hall, who should appear, but a middle aged university student teacher supervisor and her female student who would be working with "my" class in a few weeks. I explained that I was only the sub and that the teacher would probably be returning the following week. I suggested that they return then. Despite my not so subtle hints, the university supervisor was quite adamant that I allow them to observe right then and there. Opening the classroom door with a flourish, I explained that the children were in the midst of a Valentine's party they had organized. The two ladies remained in the classroom for less than two minutes. Judging from the student teacher's reaction to the party, I doubt that she remained in teaching!

After the party had finished and we cleaned up, I asked my students to level with me for a few minutes. I asked them if there was always such chaos in their class. They said that they always gave substitutes a hard time (which of course I knew as a former kid myself) and that their regular teacher never allowed most of the "shtick" they had pulled on me. Desperately wanting to learn first hand, I asked them, almost but not quite pleading with them, to explain what their teacher did differently to maintain a degree of order in the classroom. I really wanted to learn from them. One or two of the kids blurted out, "Look in the teacher's bottom desk drawer." I couldn't believe my eyes! There I found a whip, which apparently made all the difference. "She threatens to whoop us with it if we're bad," they shouted in unison. An angrier outburst I don't recall ever having heard!

One-and-a-half years and 30 credit hours after deciding to become an elementary school teacher, we moved to Connecticut, where I already had accumulated enough credit hours to teach.

Twenty-five years later I read a newspaper article about the attempts of President George H. W. Bush's administration to cut out much of the substance of the Head Start nursery/pre-school program. Only then did I realize that the very same Perry School where Debbie almost did me in was one of the first serious attempts to break down those barriers obstructing educational opportunities for poor and minority children. Not far from Debbie and the popcorn and the whoopings were, unbeknownst to me, the beginnings of the Perry Preschool program in another wing of the school. There, David Weikart, Ypsilanti Public Schools special education director, along with his colleagues, was developing a model of pre-school intervention to prevent the rage and the rampant school failure that I witnessed for one week in 1964.

Quiet: Bureaucrats at Work!

August 17th, 1977

The Superintendent of Schools was eager to begin our first elementary principals' meeting prior to the opening of the school year; he had stacks of memos and reports to distribute and a very lengthy agenda. These reports and memos had been compiled during the summer by the various curriculum directors. They would be the basis of many of the changes we would be expected to make in our schools during the upcoming year.

The Superintendent, in addition to being a Harvard graduate and a respected gentleman and educator, was very supportive of his administrative and teaching staff. He had great faith in the written word and believed that if it were written down, it would be done. I could see the relief in his face as he turned these papers over to us.

We first met with the Director of English, who had a number of reports to distribute and explain. Improving writing skills had been one of the major thrusts in the school system during the past two to three years. We had implemented a new composition program, grammar program, handwriting program, and spelling program during this period. The English Director distributed his evaluation reports based on teacher surveys and analysis of handwriting samples, and a review of the compositions of the first and tenth child in each classroom (selected from those papers that were not lost, taken home, or stashed away in the child's desk). Improvement in these areas was only fair.

However, according to his analysis of the grammar section of the Iowa Test of Basic Skills, there had been a yearly increase in the average percentile since the introduction of the new grammar workbook two years before. Unfortunately, about half of the teachers indicated that they detested the workbook for various reasons and wanted to replace it with something more interesting for the students. But the administrators present were delighted with the test results, which the Director was able to document clearly with bar graphs. Teacher recommendations would fall on deaf ears—again.

While the bar graphs showed percentile gains, I hadn't observed any particular improvement in the children's punctuation and grammar in their classroom work. My guess was that because the questions of the Iowa Test were worded and presented in a format similar to the workbook which the children used daily, our children were getting intensive practice and drill in taking the Iowa Test. What we were developing was better test-takers, not necessarily better communicators or children who could think more clearly.

Regardless of what the children may have actually learned, the administration could now document and prove what the children had supposedly learned. In many educational circles, this is called accountability. Let's not fool ourselves. This is simply bureaucracy at work, where bureaucrats trust test results far more than they trust teachers with whom they have entrusted the community's children.

I "coined" an expletive, in the early 1970s, that pretty much describes my feelings towards this approach to educating young people—BUREAUCRAP!

NOTE:
- Please excuse my terminology. However, throughout my 16 years as an elementary principal it was an easy term to keep in mind when more and more bureaucratic demands were being thrown our way. I hope I was at least partially successful in shielding teachers from "bureaucrap" so they could focus on kids.

- In my opinion, Stanford Professor Linda Darling-Hammond is one of the most articulate and sensible advocates today of school reform, authentic assessment and genuine accountability. Another gem of hers to burst the bureaucratic balloon: "Bureaucratic solutions to problems of practice will always fail because effective teaching is not routine, students are not passive, and questions of practice are not simple, predictable or standardized. Consequently, instructional decisions cannot be formulated on high then packaged and handed down to teachers."[6]

Only a Daydream

August, 1977

Relaxing on my back porch with a glass of ice tea a few weeks before the opening of the new school year, a daze comes over me like the daydreams I had gazing out of my 8th grade classroom window onto the playing fields two floors below. Only now I am the school principal fantasizing that I will close my office door two hours each day during the upcoming school year.

Two hours to contemplate freedom from the educational bureaucracy—my freedom, freedom for the teachers, the children, the parents as well as for the many other administrators who are either too sapped by the bureaucratic demands or too close to retirement, or both, not to nod in compliance.

I will instruct my secretary to tell anyone who calls or requests to see me that I'm indisposed, doing my paperwork. While the chief activity of most bureaucrats and many principals is paperwork, mine will be anti-bureaucratic paperwork. I will write down my thoughts, my dreams, my joys, my regrets.

By sharing my perspective on the pervasiveness and absurdity of bureaucracy in education, I might stand a chance of communicating my vision of education without bureaucracy to parents and teachers.

REALITY SETS IN
END OF DAYDREAM

Binding
Bureaucracy

The telephone rang as I was in the midst of hanging wallpaper; only two days remained of my summer vacation. It was the Superintendent of School's secretary. The Superintendent wanted to meet with me that afternoon if at all possible—a small emergency. In the past, a call of this nature in August meant a teacher resignation and I would have to begin interviewing teacher candidates as soon as possible in order to have a well-qualified person in the classroom by September.

To my relief, the subject of the meeting was not a teacher resignation but rather the selection of binders for the new elementary curriculum handbook. I couldn't believe that I had been called in from summer vacation for this clerical meeting. However, the Superintendent was eager for each teacher to receive a copy of the curriculum handbook at the general staff meeting in late August.

This was not just another handbook. We already had student handbooks, parent handbooks, teacher handbooks, volunteer handbooks. This new handbook promised to define and articulate the elementary curriculum once and for all. For years the Superintendent had tried to assure the parents and the Board of Education that the curriculum was the same in each school and that, regardless of where a child lived in town, he or she would receive the same quality education. This handbook was an attempt to illustrate the sameness of the curriculum town-wide.

The new handbook was the product of a typical educational bureaucracy which believes that teachers and administrators can standardize education. Supposedly, if we print and bind our educational intentions into curriculum guides, the product will ensure that all teachers are carrying out the *same* curriculum, regardless of whether or not it works or is good for children or teachers.

The Blame Game then comes into play! If the teachers fail, they can blame the curriculum, which needs to be revised, yet again. If the curriculum is standardized, the administrators can blame the teachers for not teaching the curriculum. If the teachers and curriculum are not to blame, whom then to blame: the parents for sending children who are "different" and who resist standardization.

Back to the binders. They had to be ordered that very day if they were to be delivered in time for the general staff meeting at the end of August. Hence the emergency and my daughter's half-papered bedroom wall. The Superintendent's secretary wanted to know if she should order two-, three-, or four-inch binders. We discussed the pros and cons for 30 minutes. There was concern that if the text, which presently measured 1¾ inches, were squeezed into a 2-inch binder, it would be difficult to handle and teachers would feel frustrated when using it. On the other hand, if they were presented with a three-inch binder, they might be so overwhelmed that they wouldn't attempt to read it. The Superintendent's most gracious and efficient secretary then suggested placing it in a four-inch binder, so that teachers could add other materials to it and keep it available, rather than stored in a classroom cabinet, which is the fate of most curriculum guides. I suggested that the teachers might panic if they received a half-empty binder—afraid that the second half of the curriculum was yet to come.

Seeing that a decision was not going to be made in the foreseeable future, I suggested—tongue in cheek—that each teacher be allowed to select the binder of his or her choice. As the Superintendent valued the opinions of the teachers, he thought this was a reasonable resolution. It was decided to distribute the new handbook sans binder, with a metal ring, for its debut at the meeting. Teachers would be asked to complete a binder survey (more paper-work) at the general staff meeting before leaving to prepare their classrooms for the children who would be arriving the next day.

I left the emergency binder meeting wondering what the teachers would do with their binders when they finally received them. They certainly would make great notebooks for sharing classroom collections of children's writing.

A Teacher's Plea!

Room 12
September 30, 1977

Dear Mr. L.,

Since school began three weeks ago, I have distributed 26 notices. (I have saved a copy of each in the attached manila envelope.) Although we have a student post master or mistress assigned as a class duty each week, the responsibility for seeing that the notices go out falls upon my shoulders. It becomes further complicated when a student is absent and I must remember to give him all of the notices missed while absent. I have tried to solve the problem by having a post office box for each absentee, but ...

Last week we hit a new high—ten notices in one week, with a peak on Thursday.

Monday: School Insurance notice
Tuesday: Camp Fire Girls notice
                March of Dimes Walk-a-Thon notice
Wednesday: Board of Education "Meet the Candidate" Nite notice
Thursday: Recreation Department schedule
                Announcement of Cultural Arts program—
                Mr. Slim Goodbody
                Letter from the Superintendent of Schools regarding early dismissal for October parent conferences

	October School Food Services menus
Friday:	PTO bulletin
	Permission slips for music field trip to the symphony.

All week long I have been collecting money for school pictures and payment for school insurance. Next week I shall begin by checking off permission slips for the music teacher's field trip to the symphony. If I had wanted to work for the United States Post Office, I wouldn't be in room 12 trying to teach children at a considerably lower salary than that of a postal clerk.

Last night I was so upset about the deluge of notices that I even dreamt about notices. I dreamt that I was on the playground during recess duty and all of the children were making paper airplanes out of the daily notices and flying them at me.

When I woke up from this nightmare, I decided to write this note to you. I think I have a solution, which might reduce my role as Postmistress General of Room 12. It might give us teachers a little bit more time to teach and a lot less hassle at the end of a hard day. What if the school office collected all of the notices that it received or originated during a week and sent them all out on Friday, stapled together in one sheath of paper? I could send some of my students to the office during Friday recess to help with the stapling and that would reduce my postal duties considerably.

Parents would know when to expect notices coming home and it would probably cut down on the number of lost notices. In fact, it would probably help reduce the litter on the school buses and on the streets where the children walk home as well as guarantee better informed parents.

Thank you for your attention to my plea. Please, before I lose my sanity at 3:30 each day.

Sincerely,

Postmistress General Flynn, Room 12

Memo Mania

Ludicrous memos, oppressive memos, condescending memos, offensive memos, muddled-thinking memos, verbal diarrhea memos, over-zealous memos, justifying one's job memos, covering one's self memos, and yes, at times, constructive-productive-positive memos. Memos, memos, more and more memos!

Teachers are bogged down with unnecessary bureaucratic demands, tangled up in streams of red tape, and so are sapped of valuable energy, time, and passion for teaching. How many memos does a principal or teacher receive in one year? How many actually serve to improve learning for children?

What can educators do, in the short run, in the face of the proliferation of administrative directives, requests, and guidelines? Instead of becoming annoyed or overwhelmed, instead of moving a step closer towards burnout, lighten up your day by surfing the Internet to www.mostmemorablememos.com. Enjoy some comic relief by clicking onto some of the most outrageous educational memos submitted by fellow teachers. E-mail a favorite memo you've received to www.mostmemorablememos.com for others to savor. By the simple act of adding your memo to the website, you will automatically be entered into the CRUMPLED MEMO OF THE YEAR awards competition—the CRUMMIES!

A papier-mâché statue of an outstretched forearm and a fist crumpling a batch of memos into a crinkly ball of paper, the CRUMMY, is awarded yearly in five categories:

- Most Ludicrous
- Most Wasteful of Time
- Most Pointless
- Most Unfriendly to Quality Education
- Most Positive—the Grand Winner

The administrators who originate the winning memos will each receive a CRUMMY statuette to display on their desks, or to hide away if they lack a sense of humor. All submitters and originators of award-winning memos will receive a week's holiday at a health spa to rejuvenate their spirits.

The CRUMMY AWARDS CEREMONY is televised one week prior to the traditional opening day of school in September, in time for those teacher work days and staff meetings, when an element of humor would be a most welcome relief from the order of the day. The sponsors of the CRUMMY AWARDS encourage teachers and principals to share the winning memos with fellow educators, hoping both to heighten the awareness of memo mania and to sharpen the sensitivity of administrators to the real needs of teachers—the key players in the quest for quality education for all children.

Teachers of America, you no longer need to approach your staff mailboxes with apprehension. Who knows? Your next memo may be a definite winner—a real CRUMMY. Enjoy!

Would You Let Monkeys Run the Zoo?

The Board of Education member who referred to teachers as monkeys in a zoo didn't return to the Board after my first year of teaching in town. While the extreme rudeness of his comments was certainly an exception, the Board generally listened politely and then ignored most of the views of teachers, students, and parents. They were usually heeded only when they appeared in such numbers or in such a manner as to challenge the authorities.

It is very difficult to ascertain who has the power to control the direction of a school system. Everyone thinks someone else has the authority. The children think the teachers are in charge, the teachers know that their principal is the boss, the principal is careful not to be insubordinate to the Superintendent, the Superintendent carries out the Board's directives, and the Board members think they are responding to the parents who elected them and who call their homes with complaints. Actually, the schools seem to be controlled more by bureaucracy and tradition than by persons.

Because my local board was composed of eight individuals with a wide range of educational backgrounds and philosophies, agreement by the members of the Board on a specific direction or action was rare. Furthermore, half of the Board members were newcomers or re-elected every second year, and at least one or two resigned each year because of job transfers or for personal reasons. Board members' pet projects usually died quickly once they left the Board. One member's interest in alternative schools and alternative educational approaches for children was dropped when her husband was transferred to Minneapolis. Her hours of effort had been for nothing.

Teachers and administrators spent hours one spring preparing a time study report for another Board member who was later transferred to Florida. Our task as outlined by the Superintendent was to describe the "average" school week. We recorded the number of minutes spent on each subject area and attempted to juggle everything around—a little bit here, a little bit there—to present a total of 1,776 minutes per week—certainly a very patriotic number, if nothing else. The major problem, of course, was that it was impossible to account for all the human elements that are necessarily part of the school day, and do not allow school to be bundled up neatly. We never accounted for the time used to get a drink, or to wait for a class to return from music, or to calm down after the teacher had broken up a fight in the boys' room. It didn't matter anyway, because when the report was placed on the Board agenda in September, no one could remember why the transferred Board member had requested the study in the first place!

SCHOOL
CLIMATE

We have shown that very diverse individuals, working at various educational levels, with different intellectual interests, can bring into being a learning environment in which there is responsible freedom. These facilitators of learning create a humane climate in which, being themselves real persons, they also respect the personhood of the student. In this climate there is understanding, caring, stimulation. And we have seen students respond with an avid interest in learning, with a growing confidence in self, with independence, with creative energy.

Carl R. Rogers[7]

Calming the Chaos on the Playground and in the Lunchroom

The situation in the lunchroom and on the playground during my first few years was, in plain English, chaotic! The behavior of too many children was unruly, beyond reasonble limits and at times dangerous and outrageous.

During the years of the school's early history of a laissez faire approach to children, the behavior on the playground and in the lunchroom had taken on many of the characteristics described by those who study crowd psychology. Protected by the crowd's total lack of norms and direction, the children's behavior deteriorated. When we were finally able to break down the mass mentality and reassert the role of the adults on the playground and in the lunchroom, the total school climate radically improved.

Conquering the playground

The 1st and 2nd graders used their recess to throw, kick and chase after jelly balls, play on the few available swings, race about or wander in "mini gangs" of two or three. Most of the "fun" for the boys, however, was to chase after each other or possibly grab girls' hats and tease them. This teasing was usually verbal but occasionally physical—a push here, a shove there.

Before the end of the lower grades' recess time, hordes of 3rd graders raced onto the playground from the lunchroom to capture the 1st and 2nd graders' territory. The 3rd graders organized kickball games, played 4-square and double-Dutch jump rope, and competed to see who could swing the highest and who could hang upside down on the monkey bars the longest. Unfortunately, only 10 or 15 minutes later the "big" 4th and 5th graders would come running out of the lunchroom to conquer the 3rd graders' territory, leaving the 3rd graders in fits of anger.

Playing on the playground

The firsts steps in our efforts as adults to recapture the playing fields from the crowd psychology was to make distinct noon recesses without overlapping times for the three different units. The youngsters could then have their own "territory" to play on, protected from waves of older newcomers; they now would be left alone to play "in peace."

After a few years I had somehow concluded that what the "gangs" of roaming 1st and 2nd graders really needed was a gigantic sandbox to build castles and raceways for their Matchbox cars. I asked one PTO parent who had a connection with the telephone company to donate 10 or so telephone poles to be delivered to the basically barren playground. These poles created a perfect enclosure for our new sandbox.

To my surprise, a call to the Parks Department resulted in the delivery of 12 truck-loads of sand—an instant beach. The roaming bands melted away and Matchbox play became an immediate and self sustaining hit of the non-physical kind, except to the night custodians who had to sweep up the sand from the children's sneakers each evening. Actually, the night custodians were good sports. When they occasionally complained about the extra work involved sweeping up the sand, I reminded them that we were all there, weren't we, for the benefit of the kids. Then they took it more in their stride, as they too had once been little boys.

Two 1st grade friends, Eric and Louie, set the example for establishing calm and fun on the playing fields. They spontaneously brought soccer balls to school, when it was not yet a popular children's sport in the U.S., and started kicking the balls around and developing the fanciest foot work. In fact, the entire staff was certain that they had witnessed the birth of two future Peles right there in front of their own eyes on the Independence School playing fields.

Louie and Eric continued developing their agility and stamina daily for the next few years and by the the 4th grade it became a popular noon recess game. Carl and the two Jims, beloved 4th and 5th grade teachers, also sports enthusiasts of the first order, brought organized street hockey and soft ball along with soccer to the upper grade recesses. They encouraged and welcomed everyone to join in and to play on the mixed boys and girls teams. A great feeling of camaraderie and a true sense of fair play and sportsmanship developed as a result of their determined efforts and the positive examples these three goodhearted young men set.

Lunchroom chaos

Rosina was able to mesmerize the 200 1st and 2nd graders who sat and ate quietly during her once a week lunchroom duty. Proud of her Welsh heritage, Rosina had a special love of words and a special gift. She, who had "taught a generation of 1st graders to read, hundreds of six year olds to love words, and to tell stories, and to memorize poems and to love themselves,"[8] walked about the cafeteria amongst the children for a full 20 minutes once a week with a twinkle in her eye reciting poems and rhymes to the fascination of the youngsters:

Riddle riddle ree	Riddle riddle ree
What color do I see?	What tree do I see?
It ends with an N	It starts with a P
And starts with a G.	And ends with an E.

Unfortunately, during the other days there were no "riddle riddle rees" and the teacher aides and the teachers on duty did all they could to keep the decibels down and the food from flying. Those caught with the most outlandish misdemeanors were sent to the principal. When the older students arrived for their lunch periods, things only deteriorated further. The fact that the lunchroom was a multi-purpose room designed as an auditorium, gym, and lunchroom, made matters only worse, as the acoustics were dreadful and the long rectangular folding metal tables made civil conversation almost impossible. All in all, the chaotic cafeteria was an arena as wearing for the teachers as for the children. How could a teacher teach or a child learn after being through the cafeteria wringer!

Expanding the noon hour

After having tried a number of unsuccessful approaches to establishing discipline in the cafeteria, I spent one full summer thinking about the alternatives; I was fully aware that the tenor in the lunchroom, combined with the problems on the playground, seriously impacted upon the remaining afternoon hours of classroom studies and student learning.

In September, I proposed to the teachers that we eliminate the lunchroom entirely; the children would eat in the classrooms, family style (rather than 19th century orphanage or prison style). It was a gamble and I really didn't know how the teachers might react.

I proposed extending the noon hour by 15 minutes, thereby giving the children 15-20 minutes to eat followed by a 40 minute break. Most teachers agreed to give it a try, although a few were skeptical about the feasibility of children eating in their classrooms and of the plan in general. We tried it, and after a month or so, the teachers saw that it worked and that the climate in the school had improved appreciably.

We were then able to offer a number of 40 minute NOON HOUR CHOICES for the students. By freeing up the lunchroom/gym, our P.E teacher, Connie, always updated with the most modern approaches to P. E., was able to offer a variety of physical fitness activities and cooperative games; George opened his art room and at times the photo developing lab that he had created with a PTO mini-grant; Joan, our multi talented vocal and instrumental music teacher, could schedule choruses or band or orchestra; and the school library was open to read, pursue projects, do homework, or play quiet games like chess.

Needless to say, a large number of the students on any particular day chose to go outside to the playground where the 2 Jims, upon finishing eating with their kids, daily organized street hockey or soccer or softball depending upon the weather and the conditions of our notoriously rutted back field. By offering the students and teachers TIME and CHOICE, and with the lunchroom eliminated, the NOON HOUR and atmosphere on the playground completely changed.

The commitment and caring attitude of the Independence teachers is what made it work. Till now I remember daily walking into the upper grade classrooms and seeing 15 or so street hockey sticks stacked against one corner of each classroom waiting for the noon hour when they would be gathered up by the boys and girls to play together in large numbers on the blocked-off blacktop driveway; I do not recall one accident or incident of foul play—only sportsmanship of the best kind.

Today, I'm afraid, a principal and his staff would be too intimidated to take an extra 15 minutes from the formal curriculum for a noon hour of constructive play and involvement in interests of the children's choice in fear that the standardized test scores might fall by a critical 2 or 3 percentage points (which is not necessarily true and which in the last analysis proves nothing about what the children really have learned from the formal or informal curriculum). In fact, recesses are being eliminated or shortened to give teachers more minutes to "prepare" for the barrage of testing in an effort to focus on selected test items to improve test scores—a dubious preoccupation.

NOTE:
Recently, in the summer of 2006, one of our former students, now in her mid thirties and CEO of a non profit charity which she founded, fondly recalled how she developed her love for soccer during our noon hour; and by chance years later met her husband through playing soccer as an adult. They had stopped in Jerusalem before embarking on a 6 month honeymoon journey to third world countries in order to learn more about the basic needs of the people, and how her non-profit organization could incorporate possible solutions and help people become more independent and self reliant.

If Independence School had influenced only this one idealistic young woman by a mite throughout six of her formative years, our school had touched the future.

A Welcoming and Welcome Day

September 1, 1977

As hassled as yesterday was with its administrative directives and meetings, today, the second Teacher Work Day, was low key but busy with preparations for the opening day of school and this afternoon's Open House for newcomers.

Teachers were revitalizing their empty, lifeless classrooms—bringing in plants and animals, unrolling reading and discussion corner carpets, borrowing books and book jackets from the library to brighten up their rooms and spur on new reading interests, decorating the walls with art work from the previous year's classes and ... They were becoming familiar with class lists and the names of their children, especially the new children who would be coming in this afternoon to the Open House. Bus assignments were being double checked to ensure that every child got on the right bus home on the first day—especially the 1st and 2nd graders who often forgot their bus numbers with the excitement and anxiety of the first day. Enthusiasm was at a high!

The staff broke at noon for a pot luck lunch and gathered at the home of a staff member who lived nearby. After a delicious lunch, two teachers surprised us with a

new game for the staff to play on the backyard lawn—
Hug Tag.

They had learned this game during a weeklong humanistic and personal development workshop earlier in the
summer. Some of us were a little shy to join in at first.
The rules were simple:

- You're "it" and out of the game if you're tagged
  while not hugging another person.
- Only 2 people can be hugging
- If a third person comes over, one person must find
  another person to hug.

We all became hysterical with laughter running about
the back yard randomly hugging one another trying not
to be "tagged it." While most of us had been on a first
name basis for years, a friendly hug seemed to be a real
expression of our feelings towards one another as we
began another year working closely together as a staff.

We returned to the school shortly before the kindergarteners and the children whose families were new in town
began arriving for the Open House. We were all energized
by the lunch and the camaraderie of the Hug Tag.

The school exuded a warm, personal welcoming feeling.
A PTO mother and her 4th grade daughter greeted the new
families and directed them to the classrooms and answered
questions about bus assignments, hot lunches, and all the
other things that kids worry about the first day of school. The
new kindergarteners, hand in hand with their moms and dads,
were both excited and hesitant, and were visibly relieved after
they had visited their classroom and met their new teacher.

The parent who came in to find a home for two guinea
pigs and the parent who requested to see the guidance

counselor regarding a family emergency were welcomed by the office staff. The school nurse could be seen putting up a new Star Wars poster alongside her nutrition poster.

A highlight of the afternoon for me was the invitation by Marilyn, the kindergarten bus driver, to join her and some of the kindergarteners on one of her many short rides around the neighborhood. I too felt like a kindergartener as this was a first for me after nine years of having been the school principal. Marilyn was my favorite bus driver as she cast the same spell upon the children as Captain Kangaroo or the fairy god mother in Disney's Cinderella. Marilyn, with her discarded car antenna used like an old fashioned blackboard pointer, gave several safety tips as the children waited to board the bus, each tip punctuated by waving her magical antenna in the air as if she were ready to sing Bibbidy-Bobbidy-Boo.

Something new to me was the driver's "blind spot" immediately in front of the bus which Marilyn acted out for the children who were taking turns sitting in the driver's seat. Short and spunky, Marilyn appeared and disappeared several times in front of the bus as she continued her "lecture" and safety demonstration. What a wonderful character, driver, teacher and person!

My day ended at about 4:30 with a few interviews for a special education classroom aide. One of the two candidates, whom the teacher and I fell in love with within the first five minutes, reminded us both of Mother Goose. Mother Goose began work the next day.

What a great beginning to a new school year!

"Who Owns the
School, Anyway?"

Whenever a primary grade youngster asked me in all earnestness, "Mr. Lakin, do you own the school?" it never failed to stir the youngster in me and brighten up the moment and the day. I would respond by explaining that all the moms and dads, everyone in our town, including the kids and teachers too, owned the school. This vague and unexpected reply would leave the child a little baffled. What he or she wanted to know was who really owned the school—his teacher, or me, or maybe Mr. Kittle, the custodian, who was always chatting with kids in the hallways and reminding them to take care of the school and keep it clean. Nevertheless, regardless of the unsatisfactory answer, the child would skip down the hallway towards his destination.

Truthfully, I kept asking myself the same question throughout my 16 years as principal of that, my first and last, school. However, the "principal" reply I gave those children did not exactly match the reality that I encountered when I arrived as a young novice principal in 1968. What I had found instead was a school owned by the professionals—the principal, the teachers, the curriculum directors and the central office personnel. The parents, well, they were just the parents! Don't misunderstand me; excellent teachers are the backbone of the school, however,

NO PARENTS/NO KIDS
NO KIDS/NO SCHOOLS
NO SCHOOLS/NO TEACHERS

The school is, of course, an extension of the home and family and I hoped to bridge the gap.

As I look back almost 40 years later, it appeared as if the parents' job was to send children to school and the school would take care of the rest—educating the parents' children. The school was "owned" by the professionals, well educated, well trained, creative, caring and hard working professionals. Communication between teachers and parents/parents and teachers was kept to a bare minimum and much of it had a critical, if not angry and blaming, tone.

In September 1968 I found myself at the center of an out of control school with its laissez faire approach, where aspects of the curriculum did not meet the needs of some of the children and where the social-emotional side of children's development was being neglected. Concerns such as nurturing self confidence, encouraging fair play and cooperative living, teaching responsibility for one's actions towards others and towards the feelings of others did not fit into the framework that focused primarily on the cognitive development of the children to the exclusion of just about everything else. While much progress had been made by curriculum specialists and the teachers of the school district to incorporate into the classrooms a more modern and intellectually challenging curriculum, the time had come to align the curriculum with the human factors. As one principal was fond of saying, "the tail is wagging the dog."

It was time for teachers and parents to begin a dialogue as to what was best for their individual children and the school community as well. Neither the professionals nor the parents own the school. The school exists to assist the family in educating and socializing the young child. The school cannot do the job in isolation and neither can most families, notwithstanding the homeschoolers.

During the following years a process developed whereby school and home were drawn closer together, parents participated more in their child's school and education, and a closer bond was forged between parents and teachers resulting in a greater degree of trust and goodwill. Teachers became very open to listening to parents' concerns and input, and vice versa. By listening to one another, by collaborating together for each child's benefit, a perception developed among most parents, teachers and children that it was their school—that it belonged to us all.

Staff Decision Making

The teachers on my staff were a little taken aback when, after sharing information about a number of my sabbatical visitations and Roosevelt School in particular (see Remarkably Good Fortune, page 185), I suggested organizing a few days away for the staff to discuss how they might play a greater role in our school's decision making process.

I was able to secure the funds to free the teachers. We met on the campus of a local college where we participated in sessions with two professional group trainers. At the onset of the sessions, I explained that the teachers were free to make any types of school decisions that they as a group agreed upon, with the exception of matters pertaining to pupil safety and confidentiality within our school, and personnel decisions, which at this point were solely in the hands of the Superintendent's office and the Board of Education..

After an intensive and exhilarating two days of discussions and some heated emotional exchanges, the teachers reached two conclusions:

1. They did not want to be involved in all the nitty-gritty decisions that a principal makes in the running of a school. However, they wanted to be able

to bring any matter that concerned them to the staff to discuss—with the understanding that the staff would implement any decisions made.

2. The staff recommended meeting as needed (rather than having weekly principal meetings) under the leadership of a teacher. The teacher, selected by the staff, would call meetings when teachers suggested items to be discussed at the Staff Decision Making meetings. (Administrative details would be written by the principal and distributed separately.)

The Staff Decision Making process provided teachers with a real say in matters important to them. It stimulated the discussion of concerns informally amongst the staff before deciding whether or not to bring them to the entire teaching staff. Already a close staff that communicated well with one another, they were able to resolve many concerns informally as well.

The chairperson met with me as needed to inform me of decisions taken by the staff, to share recommendations of the staff which needed to be followed up by me, or to invite me to a meeting where my input was necessary. At times, I also placed items on the Staff Decision Making agenda to be discussed.

Items discussed, to name a few, ran the gamut from issues of ***discipline and school climate*** (older children not listening to the teachers of the younger grades on the playground, children coming in at the beginning of the school day agitated by problems on the bus), ***curriculum matters*** (the overstuffed curriculum, fostering integrated studies, the lack of sufficient in-service training for new

or updated school system mandated programs, incorporating creative dramatics into the reading program and
environmental awareness into the life of the school), and
school organization (better utilization of the library for
classroom research projects, reassignment of school para-
professional aides for classroom support).

The Staff Decision Making process became an integral part of our school life: teachers listening to teachers,
principal listening to teachers, teachers listening to principal, all facilitated by a high level of openness and trust
empowering staff to collaborate more freely.

BUILDING A HOME-SCHOOL PARTNERSHIP

**Independence Elementary School:
A 15 Year Perspective**

Our school developed a reputation in the 1970s and 1980s as a school where teachers truly listened to parents and parents reciprocated—where the level of trust spiraled upwards and developed its own momentum.

It wasn't always that way!

Breaking the Barrier of Distrust

During my first years as principal of Independence Elementary School in the late 1960s, I encountered an invisible curtain of distrust drawn between segments of the parent body and the staff. Certainly there were parents who supported their children's teachers and welcomed me as their new principal. There were many—the extremely welcoming and positive PTO board, devoted library volunteers, and many other moms and dads who communicated their interest in contributing to the welfare of the school.

However, a great number of parents distanced themselves from the school only to attend twice yearly parent-teacher conferences or to telephone the teacher or principal regarding a school problem their child might be experiencing.

During its brief six year history, it appeared that the administrators of Independence School felt that it was solely the school's job to educate the children, and signaled to the parents that they needn't be involved with nor interfere in the business of the school. Once this dysfunctional relationship between home and school became clear to me, I knew I had an unexpected challenge ahead of me—to find ways of breaking down the barrier of distrust while building a close home-school partnership.

Even as I type this almost 40 years later, I feel pangs in my stomach thinking about the hostility and anger generated by a dozen or so parents with an intense and extreme distrust of the school. They lashed out at their children's school in a variety of ways—bad mouthing teachers, criticizing school discipline and attacking the curriculum whenever and wherever they could, in an effort to enlist support of other parents in their private battle against the school.

So I embarked on a campaign to point out to teachers and parents alike the necessity of building a true home-school partnership for the benefit of every single child. At first, some teachers were reluctant to be more open to parents, either through lack of experience or because of having been "burned" once too often by parents with very abrasive demands or with an axe to grind. I reassured teachers I would totally support them as long as they respected each child's individual needs as a learner and as a person. Respect of individual children, staff members and parents was to be the foundation of our relationships, our educational programs, and our future as we worked together forging a school community.

I sent an unmistakable message to the parent body that their new principal intended to open channels of communication and to foster positive relations with the school community. Children needed to feel the security of the rapport between school and home, rather than to be confused by an undercurrent of tension between teachers and parents.

I spoke at our September general PTO meeting, at grade level open houses, and at neighborhood coffee evenings graciously hosted by different families. To facilitate and simplify communications between parents and teachers, we encouraged parents to drop in or to telephone teachers 20 minutes before or after the school day. A Friday Bulletin was inaugurated to keep families informed about school events, policies and special classroom programs. A few of the younger teachers began sending home marvelous weekly classroom newsletters (pre personal computer, pre EdGate/SchoolNotes.Com.)

From the first days, weeks, months and years, the PTO presidents and the many committee chairpersons and volunteers actively supported the school in a host of ways. Most importantly, they were advocates of the school who paved the way for closer communications between parents and the school. Whether it was welcoming new families to the school community or supporting teachers through mini-grants for special classroom projects; bringing Artists-in-Residence to work directly with classes and small groups of children or buying new equipment for the school, these and other activities, such as the yearly spring Fun Fair, all contributed towards improving home-school relations and ultimately helped the school to become a more positive learning environment.

I sat in on as many parent-teacher conferences as possible to become better acquainted with the children, their parents and teachers. By the end of the second year I was quite well acquainted with almost every child from the 1st grade and above. While visiting classrooms, I observed the quality of the children's learning and spotted those children who might be lagging behind, those needing more of a challenge, and those experiencing some sort of difficulty. Moreover, I reassured both the children and their teachers that they had not only a principal in the school office but also a friend who cared about them and who would be fair in helping them solve school problems.

My basic message to parents was that our doors were open; any concern related to their child's education was also a concern of ours. We encouraged parents to contact us and we reassured them we would keep them abreast of what was going on with their children. (Nothing is more rightly infuriating to a parent than finding out that a problem has existed for a long a period of time without their knowledge. "Why didn't you tell us before, we could have done something about it if we had only known!")

Furthermore, I tried to convey my very strong conviction that parents know their children better than anyone else and therefore parents needed to play a vital role in assisting the school in educating their children. Most parents accepted what we were trying to communicate at face value, while some wondered whether these "words" were just more educational jargon. Here and there a parent or two remained trapped in past battles with the school (or with themselves) and simply refused to accept our invitation to participate in the life of their child's school.

In response to a parental survey, it became clear that a large number of parents wanted to see more of the "paperwork" children were doing in math, reading, composition and so on. Most teachers kept folders of children's papers as ONE means of tracking progress. In response, I decided unilaterally that teachers would send home monthly portfolios of children's work for parents to review. As this was quite time consuming and cumbersome, the following year we limited it to the months when there were no parent conferences, and finally this practice was dropped when parents, teachers and I realized it was more productive to communicate with one another as needed and to share children's written work less formally and more spontaneously—in forms such as class booklets, student diaries, classroom presentations ... I never ceased to be amazed at the myriad ways teachers were able to creatively share the work of their students.

Recognizing that the school program needed to become more transparent, we invited parents to spend a morning with their child in the classroom. Most parents were unable to do so because of work schedules or other time commitments; however, those that did come in generally left with a more positive attitude towards the educational program and a heightened respect for their children's teachers. Teachers began to feel less intimidated by parents in the classroom, and parents began to understand that an open door policy was just that, neither hollow words nor a public relations strategy.

By my third or fourth year at school, as teachers and parents got to better know one another, and many were now even on a first name basis, parents were being welcomed into classrooms as volunteers to assist teachers, especially in the lower grades. The school was no longer under a siege mentality and teachers sensed the support of the school community.

When Teachers Listen to Parents and Parents Listen to Teachers

Building upon earned trust

In order to fully focus upon the needs of children, it is imperative that teachers and parents truly **listen** to each other with open minds and open hearts. This of course requires a high level of **trust** as well as the willingness to listen to concerns that one party or another might find discomforting and disquieting. Moreover, a certain degree of caring for the "other" is a prerequisite if people are to listen to each other with understanding and empathy.

I recall in my early years sitting in on some teacher-parent conferences which were more akin to a client meeting with his or her banker. Information was exchanged, questions were raised and answered and that was that. Neither teacher nor parent was able to zero in on the essence of the child. I'm sure both adults left the meeting with an empty, if not hostile feeling, not quite understanding what really had transpired. What a pity!

As the level of trust grew, teachers and parents were going beyond exchanging statements and comments, and were beginning to probe further into what the other was really trying to communicate about the child. They were **truly listening** to each other!

Parents felt more comfortable sharing their satisfactions or concerns about the child's school program, in addition to relevant information about the child's home life. Important bits and pieces about the child were revealed that could help the teacher personalize her relationship with the child or tailor aspects of the curriculum to the child—the youngster's interests, his fears, her previous school experiences, his friendships, the comic books collection which he read and reread, her success on the girls basketball team, and so on.

Parents were also more willing to listen to the advice of the teacher or principal, who may have suggested ways to encourage a child to read more at home or stressed the necessity of limiting TV and establishing an earlier bedtime. Proposing that the parent invite a particular classmate home for after school play might be just the right remedy to help a lonely child.

Parents also felt freer to offer more personal information which might help the teachers to better motivate or connect to their child:

- "She loves to sketch animals in her free time."
- "He hates fantasy stories, but adores Garfield."
- "She writes little plays at home and puts her younger brothers in all the parts; actually she loves being the boss."
- "He could be a stand-up comedian someday—he is so funny and so quick on his feet."

- "She doesn't understand why there was slavery in America. Will you be studying African-American History this year?"

Furthermore, parents became less uptight about giving "tips" to the teachers to consider—suggestions they thought might improve instruction for their child, enrich the classroom or even clarify a situation the teacher might not be fully aware of. A handful of these generally constructive "tips" come to mind:

- "I think Sam is beginning to be turned off by so much math homework. Isn't it possible to cut the practice examples in half?"
- "Mrs. Gardner read a great book to her class which you might like to read to yours. It's by Julie Andrews Edwards of Mary Poppins' fame and is called *The Last of the Really Great Whangdoodles.*"
- "Are you aware that some of the boys feel you are unfair and call on the girls more often. Maybe you could discuss it with them?"
- "I work for the telephone company and can arrange a conference call with the whole class and one of their favorite authors." (In the early 1980s Maurice Sendak agreed to be interviewed and shared how his childhood fears and nightmares influenced the creation of *Where the Wild Things Are.*)

The invisible curtain of distrust had indeed been lifted! A true parent-teacher partnership was developing for the benefit of the children and a committed home-school partnership pervaded the life of our school. Our focus was on the individual child, the major beneficiary of the positive energy generated between home and school, parent and teacher. Moreover, everyone was a winner—the children, the parents, the teachers, the supportive staff, the principal and the community. There were no losers! It was a win-win cycle of advocacy and support in contrast to the defeatism and negativity which characterized the earlier years of our school, and reigns yet in many schools which still operate upon the "we-they" adversarial model.

Exploring Parent Involvement and Parent Participation

(1975-1984)

Remarkably good fortune

The moment I entered the "school office" of the Roosevelt Elementary School in Louisville, Kentucky, I knew that people, not bureaucracy, were at the core of the school. It was April 1975 and I had taken a 5-month sabbatical leave to research and visit communities and schools where people were exploring ways to encourage greater parent and community participation in the schooling of their youngsters. I had hypothesized that as parents and community members developed a greater connection and feeling of ownership of their local school(s), they would assume more responsibility for the success of the educational enterprise.

When I drove up to the Roosevelt School, housed in an 1867 Civil War building in the midst of an inner city racially-mixed neighborhood, I was taken aback by the poverty of the surroundings. My almost panicky first reaction was to wonder what relevance this situation would have for me and my affluent Connecticut suburban school and school district.

What I witnessed when I opened the door of the school office has remained with me to this day. As I stepped in and saw 10 or so people busy at work, I tried to identify who might be the secretary or the principal or a teacher so that I could introduce myself. But it was very unclear to me who was who. However, a moment later, a slight, casually dressed woman approached me and introduced herself as so and so, the chairperson of the Roosevelt School Board and the mother of three children in the school.

I waited about 15 minutes to meet Car Foster, the principal, who had been meeting with a parent. I explained to him that I had read about Louisville's experimental plan to create Neighborhood School Boards which empowered parents to make major educational decisions such as "determining school philosophy, ... selecting curriculum, and interviewing and recommending the hiring of teachers;"[9] in particular, I had read about his work at Roosevelt. Despite arriving on the scene unannounced, I was greeted warmly and made most welcome during my one week visitation.

When I drove away from the Roosevelt Neighborhood School five days later, I realized my mind had been blown wide open. I looked forward to the two-day 800-mile drive home to toss about the implications of what I had just observed.

For me, the concept and the actuality of the Roosevelt Neighborhood School remains a beacon of inspiration, giving direction to those who are either lost in the bureaucratic quagmire or looking for their way out of the current state of the educational establishment's dilemma. More tests, more money, more accountability and control from above, more pressure, more finger pointing and more school programs which grossly fail the undereducated urban poor and minorities are clearly not the answers. These are misguided and regressive bureaucratic solutions, in addition to being oversimplifications; they are not pathways toward school improvement, neither on the individual school level nor nationwide.

The upshot of my Roosevelt School experience was the recognition that my basic intuition was correct: by trusting and empowering people—parents, teachers, administrators and students—to assume more responsibility for the educational process and outcomes, many of the obstacles facing our schools today could be overcome

Parents' Point of View

The Parents' Point of View was an outgrowth of my sabbatical leave. I wanted to develop a "friendly" mechanism by which all parents could have greater input into their children's education. Mulling this over for a few weeks, I decided to create a short open-ended questionnaire for parents to complete at the end of the school year. I called it the Parents' Point of View. And that's exactly what it was. As parents are concerned, most of all, about the quality of their own children's schooling, the Parents' Point of View gave them an opportunity to evaluate their child's year and to provide input into the following year's program for each of their children. It consisted of two questions:

- In what ways has this been a "growth" year for your child at school?
- What major goals would you like next year's teacher to work towards with your child? Which goals would you like next year's teacher particularly to emphasize?

The purpose of the Parents' Point of View was twofold:

Firstly, it provided feedback to the child's current teacher as it was returned directly to the teacher—a form of evaluation of the child's school year. Also, it provided feedback to me as I carefully read each parent's response in order to better understand each child. (Very few parents chose not to return the Point of View.)

Secondly, the Parents' Point of View was given to the following year's teacher to assist in planning for the child's new school year. In addition, information garnered from the Points of View in May and June was helpful in sensitively placing children with teachers and groups of children for the following school year. The teachers and I tried to place children with teachers and classroom structures that we felt would be most fitting and challenging for them. We weren't always able to make a match, but I believe we were quite successful.

I cannot emphasize enough how moved I was by the great care that parents took to describe their children as well as by the high level of trust exhibited by the teachers.

Furthermore, a purpose was served that I had not fore-seen: it provided yet another opportunity for parents (and teachers) to look carefully at their children both as learn-ers and as youngsters developing during those "magic years" of the elementary grades.

While writing this piece I found the following two Parents' Points of View amongst the mementoes and mis-cellaneous papers I had saved these many years. They are an accurate example of the thoughtful and constructive comments parent-after-parent wrote year-after-year for nine years (1976-1984). Although most were quite posi-tive about the child's progress or the teacher's program, they were written, almost without exception, in a helpful manner and served to advance the overall quality of edu-cation in our school.

INDEPENDENCE SCHOOL
May, 1982
PARENTS' POINT OF VIEW

In what ways has this been a "growth" year for your child at school?

Donna was very "young" when she started 1st grade, probably because she was somewhat babied at home. To support the teacher's effort in school our family worked with Donna and encouraged her to do more things for herself. She began changing rapidly and began to work hard to show us how well she could do. It became very important for her to learn to read and to count change. She took pride in knowing sight words and learning to spell. She's still somewhat insecure and worries a lot, but she is happier with herself and school than she was last year.

What major goals would you like next year's teacher to work towards with your child?
Which goals would you like next year's teacher particularly to emphasize?

I'd like the teacher to know that she does struggle with new work and needs patience. She gets upset easily. I think she'll come along well with reading, but may require more practice with handwriting. It takes longer for her to grasp the math work also.

My major goal for Donna would be to help her gain self-confidence and not to panic when she feels nervous. Donna's a hard worker and she will learn even if it requires extra help. I would like to see her receive positive encouragement.

Child's Name: Donna Taylor **1981-82 Grade Level: 1**
Your Signature: Lucille Taylor
(Please return this to school with your child or by mail by Tuesday, June 1, 1982.)

INDEPENDENCE SCHOOL
May, 1982
PARENTS' POINT OF VIEW

In what ways has this been a "growth" year for your child at school?

Allison is a very happy child this year. I attribute her success and growth to her teacher. We are thrilled with Allison's progress and her attitude toward people and activities. She has become more assertive and self confident. She's enthusiastic about trying new things and will stick with a new activity until she has achieved her goal or until the activity ends. Beside her school work, Allison has become involved with swimming, singing, dancing and gymnastics—which all have been rewarding for her. She's developing into a fine person and we're extremely proud of her.

What major goals would you like next year's teacher to work towards with your child?
Which goals would you like next year's teacher particularly to emphasize?

Allison needs affection and encouragement. If she feels secure in her relationship with her teacher, she excels. Allison will seek out extra work and ask for direction if the teacher will show her friendliness.

I think she feels lacking in mathematics. It takes her longer to retain this type of information or learning. We are willing to work with her at home if need be.

Child's Name: Allison Adler   **1981-82 Grade Level:** 3
Your Signature: Katherine Adler
(Please return this to school with your child or by mail by Tuesday, June 1, 1982.)

ENVISIONING THE FUTURE

The illiterate of the 21st century will not be those who cannot read and write, but those who cannot learn, unlearn, and relearn.

Alvin Toffler

I have never let my schooling interfere with my education.

Mark Twain

Beyond the Three 'R's!

The 21st century school is a caring learning community

WHERE: The **FOCUS** is on **the INDIVIDUAL CHILD'S RIGHT** to develop intellectually, social-emotionally and academically to his or her fullest capacity under the guidance of well educated, highly trained, dedicated and well paid professional teachers.

WHERE: **PARENT(S)** are recognized as major players in the child's overall development and are actively encouraged to participate in all aspects of the life of the child and school and in major educational decisions such as alternative programming and/or alternative schooling.

WHERE: All the adults in the school community are **CHILD ADVOCATES** and do make a difference for children.

WHERE: All those in positions of authority (teachers, principals....) **LEAD WITH THEIR HEARTS** as well as with their minds.

WHERE: Building bridges between school and home leads to maximum levels of **CONFIDENCE** and **TRUST.**

WHERE: Ongoing two-way **COMMUNICATION** (people truly listening to one another) minimizes conflict and maximizes understanding and creative problem solving.

WHERE: All members are **ENERGIZED** through **ACTIVE PARTICIPATION.**

WHERE: Bureaucratic regulations and demands are minimized in order to maximize **INITIATIVE** and **CREATIVITY.**

WHERE: **RESPECT, KINDNESS, FAIRNESS,** and **COOPERATIVE LIVING** are taught as basic values of the school community.

WHERE: **PROBLEM SOLVING and CONFLICT RESOLUTION** are intentionally taught within the school-laboratory.

WHERE: **PLAY** and **IMAGINATION** are recognized as key elements in childhood and growth and are incorporated into the curriculum and school life.

WHERE: **MUSIC** and the **ARTS** enhance the **SOUL** and the **SPIRIT** of the school community and encourage children to express their inner selves.

WHERE: The harmony between the child's
PHYSICAL, MENTAL, and
EMOTIONAL FITNESS is furthered by
offering a balance of both cooperative and
competitive play and individual and team
sports before, during and after the regular
school day.

WHERE: An expression of a wide range of
FEELINGS and **EMOTIONS** is accepted
as normal and an integral part of the child's
development and enriches the child's daily
school life.

WHERE: **AGGRESSION** is **REDIRECTED**
into positive activity and the flip side
of positive is not negativity but rather
ENCOURAGEMENT.

WHERE: **TECHNOLOGY** is embraced to
ENHANCE the child's individual **STYLE
of LEARNING,** and to **FURTHER** the
child's **UNDERSTANDING** of the complexities of our rapidly changing world.

**DEDICATED TO
THE INDEPENDENCE SCHOOL STAFF**

Big School and
Small School

Summer, 1978

My ideal school is a small school with fewer than 150 children. In a small school, communications are simple and relationships informal. I have been the principal of Big School and Small School for the past five years. Big School has about 500 children and 25 staff members, whereas Small School has 125 children and six staff members.

Small School does not need a principal. When I visit Small School twice a month, I know that education is the main order of the day. The teachers are not burdened with daily mimeographed notices, attendance lists, duty schedules, revised schedules, and all of the other paperwork that emanates daily from a principal's office, nor with the endless organized meetings to bring staff members together, as they have many daily opportunities to communicate informally with one another for the benefit of kids.

Still, Small School does have a leader, a very fine leader. She is a teacher—a head teacher. Most of her time is in the classroom with children. An experienced and talented teacher, Mary Ann teaches a 1st-2nd grade classroom with the help of a part-time teacher, who frees her up to consult with teachers and parents and to carry out other school-wide duties. Mary Ann provides the leadership to help 125 children and six teachers to work together as an educational community—a school.

When I share my vision about small schools, people always ask what I suggest we do with all the expensive and large school buildings that have been constructed. My answer is to house two, four, or more small schools in the big school buildings (or "facilities" as they are referred to by central office administrators). Is this not a simple solution to untangling schooling from the complexities of the "economy of scale"? Teachers could then get on with the job of teaching—connecting with children: motivating them, inspiring them, challenging them, and providing them with the basic foundation and love for a lifetime of learning.

NOTE:

When I wrote this piece 27 years ago not only was I convinced, as I am still today, that "small is beautiful," but also I had been becoming increasingly concerned by the trend I had observed to build larger and larger school buildings. It was the belief of many authorities in public education and town and city government that larger "facilities" would, by themselves, offer improved educational opportunities, not recognizing the consequences of massing larger and larger numbers of young persons into more and more anonymous settings—some would say war zones.

These emerging educational edifices, these palaces of learning, were often rationalized by the decision-makers as benefiting from the "economy of scale." However, to those of us on the sidelines they often appeared to be erected as ego trips for competing architectural firms and for certain school administrators, Board of Education and Building Committee members filled with awe at their own achievements.

A quarter of a century later, numerous educators, private foundations and local communities are acting upon the recognition that smaller school units are more humane, practical, and suited to the enterprise of learning. One need only look at the experience of New York City during the past 5 years. In 2003 the Bill & Melinda Gates Foundation gave $51 million to support 67 new small high schools to "prepare underserved students for success in today's demanding economy." In 1992 The Julia Richman High School of 3000 students had a 1/3 graduation rate while ten years later it had became the Julia Richman Educational Complex (JREC) housing four small alternative high schools with graduation and college acceptance rates approaching 80%.[10] Small size alone does not create challenging and high quality education that places young people first; however, the proper environment is needed in which professional teachers, administrators and involved families and community members can nurture and truly educate adolescents through their critical years of growth.

Mining the Minds
of All of Our
Youth

MINING MINDS requires that we rethink schooling from the perspectives of both TIME and RELEVANCY. As much time as possible needs to be devoted to educating children with minds wide open, stretching and expanding their thinking skills while fostering an eagerness to tackle challenging questions and issues and to address problems calling for solutions. **All** of our nation's youth need to be given the opportunities whereby their potentialities are **genuinely** nurtured, their innate curiosity and creativity awakened and their achievement levels maximized in preparation for satisfying, creative and productive lives.

Public schools as we know them were first organized during the industrial revolution and functioned as day care for the children of those working in the factories, and to provide those very same children with a limited range of skills to enable them to enter the workforce. In a certain manner, our concept of schooling and learning (**MINDING** MINDS) has not significantly changed.

The traditional school, as it now exists, has too much built-in wasted and counterproductive time. Ask any teacher or pupil and she or he could enumerate the wasted minutes spent waiting for a class to come to order, dealing with disruptive students, focusing on aspects of the curriculum that are irrelevant or outdated, and so forth. In many schools children are still being assigned excessive amounts of busy work to fill up time while their minds are being minded.

In many classes, there are children who sit passively tuned out, or who are confused while "listening" to full class presentations, or are too shy or too bored to participate. The "brain drain" begins the moment a youngster recognizes that his or her waking hours could be better spent on more challenging pursuits, some legal, others not, beyond the classroom door.

In the teen years, school violence and involvement with alcohol and drugs are often symptomatic of the alienation some of our youth feel in depersonalized classes and institutions. Wasting minds and allowing the potentialities of significant numbers of our youth to remain undeveloped is neglect of outrageous and staggering proportions. Linda Darling-Hammond chillingly describes, in *Many Children Left Behind*, the tragedy of greater and greater numbers of students leaving school with only a seventh or eighth grade education, rather than being prepared to join the workforce: "These students join what is increasing known as a 'school-to-prison pipeline' carrying an increasing number of undereducated youth almost directly into the criminal justice system."[11]

How can we best use TIME to the advantage of our students—to **mine** minds? My experience during the past 40 years reaffirms again and again that the learning that "sticks" comes in situations where students are so highly motivated that you cannot stop them from moving forward. Motivation through tests and grades results in "covering" the curriculum, if even that, not in the thirst for exploring further, directly or tangentially.

Much more choice time needs to be build into our students' school day and week, to harness their physical and intellectual powers; choice time whose magnetic force and attraction is based upon the **intrinsic** interest of the specific matter of study or the match with the **personal** interests and curiosity of the particular child or teen. When the teaching profession is given more authority to make decisions for kids, I am convinced that both individual teachers and collaborative groups of teachers will come up with the proper matches, given, of course, adequate training and time alongside both financial and moral support.

A few examples should suffice as the possibilities abound:

High school biology

Recently I became aware of high school biology courses that capitalize on the interest of students in **forensics,** an interest spurred on by the popularity of the many TV detective shows and movies that have used forensics in their criminal investigations. These courses can provide a highly motivating option to many youngsters who find the traditional approach to studying high school biology futile. (See *Teaching Cell Biology to Nonscience Majors Through Forensics, or How to Design a Killer Course* by

Laura Atwood, Department of Biology, Marist College, 3399 North Road, Poughkeepsie, New York 12601[12])

Focused small group instruction

For 18 years Karen and I taught ESL (English as a Second Language) in Jerusalem to small groups of five youngsters each in our private alternative English center, The Learning Alternative. The students participated in these afternoon classes by choice for **one** full hour a week for 30 weeks per year. The instructional power of these small groups was extremely gratifying while not totally unexpected. The students progressed at least **twice** as fast in their mastery and enjoyment of the English language (understanding, speaking, reading and writing) in **one-third** the amount of hours of the regular school English classes.

I propose that schools consider integrating Focused Small Group Instruction as one of the basic components of their school program. Children would be able to master the "basic" curriculum in considerably less time than at present and with a much higher degree of breadth and depth. These Focused Small Group Instructional classes should not be viewed as remedial classes attempting to pick up the pieces of past failures, but rather as basic developmental classes. The additional hours freed up for children could be used to provide challenging options to **mine** the minds and open the hearts of all our youth.

(See Appendix II, which describes the attributes which I believe led to the success of our Focused Small Group English Instruction.)

Fortunately, there is much good news on the scene as educators, community activists, and philanthropists have begun, since the early 2000s, to form partnerships to seriously evaluate, rethink, and implement programs that address themselves to many of the above mentioned concerns. Very recently an e-mail came across my desk from the Bill & Melinda Gates Foundation pinpointing the work being done in partnership with the Green Dot Public Schools in the Los Angeles Unified School District (LAUSD) to create "high quality high schools that provide students with **a new '3Rs'**: rigor, relevance and relationships—a **rigorous** curriculum for all students, **relevant** classes, and meaningful **relationships** with adults who support all students to achieve at higher levels."

The Green Dot Schools are built upon the following Six Tenets of High Performing Schools developed by the Los Angeles based Small School Alliance:

1. **Small Schools:** All schools should be 500 students or less;
2. **High Expectations for All Students:** Every student will take a rigorous curriculum. All high school students will have a college-prep curriculum that meets the University of California/California State University A-G requirements for college entrance;
3. **Local Control:** Increase local control so that critical decisions at each school, including

budgets and personnel, are made on-site and by school principals and teachers;

4. **Get Dollars into the Classroom:** Shift school revenues away from central administration and toward teachers. Teachers should be paid more and be granted increased input into key policy decisions such as curriculum selection and elective classes;

5. **Parent Participation:** Demand greater parental participation by requiring that families of students dedicate at least 30 hours annually to their child's/children's education experience (through volunteering, tutoring at home, etc.); and

6. **Keep Schools Open Later:** Schools will be kept open until at least 5 p.m. during school days to accommodate the schedules of working families and the needs of the community at large.[13]

What is also most heartening and hopeful is the constructive role that many philanthropic foundations are playing in the re-creation of the American public school. The work of the Bill & Melinda Gates Foundation is one striking example. Not unlike the work of Andrew Carnegie who first began funding free public libraries promoting self-education in the 1880s, the Bill & Melinda Gates Foundation, "to this date has invested **$1 billion** to improve high schools, including supporting the creation of more than 1,100 high-quality high schools in 42 states and the District of Columbia. Since 2003, the foundation has invested about $30 million in the Los Angeles region to open new high schools and strengthen existing ones."[14]

When our public schools make that final leap and switch their mind-set from **Minding Minds** to **Mining Minds** and challenge **all** youngsters to become the best they can be, choosing from a broad spectrum of studies that suit their personal interests and goals, the results might very well be a renaissance of public education in our nation.

I am optimistic. I sense that the "tipping point" is within reach and that the new generation is preparing to illuminate a fundamentally changed reality of educational opportunity for **all** of our youth.

Dynamic Principals Plus Dynamic Principles

The Whitman Corporation placed an advertisement in the Fall 1990 Newsweek Special Educational issue, which rang true to me as an educator. What the Whitman Company stated in their ad seemed, and still seems, like plain old simple common sense to the principal and teacher in me.

And in 2006, USA Today published an article about principal Jeffrey Robinson of the Baltimore Talent Development High School. According to reporter Gregg Toppo, Robinson also has a simple common-sense approach. What the Whitman Corporation learned 16 years ago and principal Jeffrey Robinson is committed to today, seem to have clear implications for the schools of the present and future. Compare them and draw your own conclusions:

"Here's What We've Learned." (Whitman Corporation advertisement)

We've learned that good management makes the difference, in education as in business.

Each year, Whitman Corporation gives a $5,000 cash award to each of the 20 best Chicago Public School principals who can spend it on any school project of their choice. As we've selected the winners, we've learned that the best schools are not the result of their racial or ethnic makeup, their location in the city, the money spent per pupil (although it's obviously important), the number of students per class, or the age of the buildings.

The best schools are invariably the ones with the best managers. The best principals have several common attributes. They care deeply about their students. They know them by name. They maintain discipline, and encourage respect. They motivate their teachers. They consult with parents. They fight for supplies and equipment. They have great courage and a lot of love. And it shows.

To a surprising degree, their students don't drop out. They don't do drugs. They study and learn. Their test scores are high. Lots of them go on to college. They're not all perfect. But they're a lot better than the average.

So as the nation seeks answers to the education crisis, please consider what we've learned in our modest program. Look to the principals. We're really proud of our Whitman Award winners. They've made a difference in Chicago.[15]

Principal Jeffrey Robinson (USA Today 9/28/06)

Baltimore Talent Development High School ... has no admissions requirements. Students are admitted by lottery. The school day is no longer than most: Students arrive at 9 a.m. and leave at 3:50 p.m. It doesn't have a football team or marching band. It doesn't even have gym class.

Yet it's working, on a simple, common-sense principle: Find a dynamic principal with high expectations, give him what he needs, and let him hire the teachers he wants. Provide a rigorous curriculum and massive intervention for freshmen who read and do math at elementary school levels. And then get out of the way ...

Robinson shrugs when asked about the school's secret formula: "It's just an ordinary school that has expectations."[16]

What do you think? Do these words ring true to you?

Planting Schools

Envisioning America's educational landscape

The future of the K-12 American educational landscape is clear in my mind's eye. I envision tens of thousands of **smaller caring public schools of choice** planted throughout the land by teachers, parents and community members who recognize that America's strength lies in its diversity, its creativity, its ingenuity, and in its commitment to democracy and quality education *for all.*

If one takes a careful look at the diversity of post secondary educational institutions dotting our 50 states, one can see a mirror image of what our K-12 educational horizon has the potential of becoming: a wide spectrum of schools providing abundant choices for students and their families—pluralistic schools for a pluralistic America.

These **smaller caring public schools of choice** inspire teachers, students, and parents alike to assume greater "ownership" in the quality and scope of classroom programming. In addition, alongside mastering the "basics," young people have more options to exert their creative force to delve into the arts, humanities, sciences or other areas of personal interest. The possibilities are potentially as diverse as the interests and needs of the communities and clientele that these schools serve.

Furthermore, these **smaller caring public schools of choice** bear special fruit, for they are being planted upon fertile ground for developing character, commitment and camaraderie. In these more caring learning communities, people are more apt to listen to one another and to respond to each other's concerns and feelings—to one's humanity.

Many pioneers have been establishing these new **smaller caring public schools of choice,** some for as long as two decades. They are our modern day Johnny Appleseeds—the countless prime movers and leaders of the burgeoning numbers of "schools within schools," magnet schools, alternative schools, and charter schools taking root throughout the nation. Among these pioneers are well-known educational and community activists such as:

- Deborah Meier (founder of the Central Park East Secondary School in East Harlem and founder and principal of the Mission Hill K-8 School in Roxbury, MA),
- Ted Sizer (founder of the Coalition of Essential Schools),
- Dennis Littky and Elliot Washor (founders of The Big Picture Company which "believes that schools must be personalized, educating every student equally, ONE STUDENT AT A TIME"[17]), and
- Bill & Melinda Gates (whose charitable fund has donated, in NYC and Chicago alone, more than $100 million to develop **smaller public high schools of choice**).

As clearly evidenced by failure over many decades, educational bureaucracies are unable to improve local schools by superimposing top heavy, distant solutions upon schools and teachers at the local level. This approach simply does not work.

Policymakers need to set the conditions for individual schools to *evolve* rather than to burden them with excessive state and federal bureaucratic regulations. What teachers and children do **not** need is quality control by "remote control" management from government technocrats or textbook and testing publishing houses.

In sharp contrast, local, state and federal governmental units need to earmark sufficient funds to support and monitor the development of responsive, highly effective **smaller caring public schools of choice;** schools where the untapped potential of *all* young people, coupled with high expectations, will be fully realized.

This is my vision.

Appendix I

Question and Answer Booklet for Parents Independence School–Open Unit 1971–1972

What is open education?

In its simplest terms, "open" refers to the relationship between teacher and child, to choices available to the child and to open-endedness in the curriculum.

What is the Intern Program?

The interns are fully certified, first year teachers who are enrolled in a Master's Degree program in Open Education at the University of Connecticut. As Interns, they are under direct supervision of the two classroom teachers and the school principal and will receive six credits for their Internship experience at Independence School.

Each of the two Interns is a homebase teacher working closely with one half of the 3rd graders (approximately fourteen children) while participating in all of the other duties and responsibilities of a classroom teacher.

How are our children grouped?

There are 75 children in the open unit, divided approximately equally between grades 2, 3 and 4. The children begin each day in a homebase grouping with children of their grade level. The children work individually or in small groups for the majority of the day. At times children return to homebase or work in large group situations (French, music, gym etc.).

How is our day organized?

Each child begins the day in his homebase, planning his daily activities with his homebase teacher. It is the homebase teacher who is responsible for the overall progress of the child throughout the year. The remainder of the day is divided into 2 large blocks for work in the 4 major areas of the unit—communications (Room 14), math (Room 14A), science-social studies (Room 15) and art (Room 16). Time is allotted at the end of each work block to discuss activities and to share with one another. The day is not divided into periods of time devoted to particular subject areas. Instead children pursue their interests within and between disciplines in a workshop atmosphere.

What are some of the goals for our children?

Our major goal is to help each child develop in as many directions as possible within the school setting in order that each child may become what he has the potential to become. This includes:

- helping children to develop skills and to experience success and pleasure in the total school curriculum
- helping children to develop self-confidence, self-direction and self discipline
- helping children to set personal standards and to use freedom responsibly
- strengthening children's intellectual curiosity
- fostering positive attitudes toward self and school

How does the staff view the child?

The following views about how children learn and grow are those to which the unit teachers and the principal are firmly committed:

- A child's growth potential is maximized in an accepting and trusting environment.
- Individual differences must be accepted, valued and encouraged if all children are to become healthy adults.
- Children have a natural desire to learn and to succeed and that, given appropriate opportunity, they will do so responsibly.
- Children learn best in an environment which is more active than passive, more integrated than isolated and in an environment which is rich in varied materials for independent pursuit.

- Children do not have the same timetable for learning and growth. The teacher is sensitive to the child's readiness to move to the "new" as well as to consolidate the "old."

What is the relationship between teacher and child?

The relationship between teacher and child is informal with all channels of communication open. Because the teacher is able to view the child as he is in many different real situations, he has more information with which to help the child learn and grow.

What kind of structure does the teacher provide?

There are a number of ways in which the teacher structures the open classroom.

A rich and varied environment is developed so children are invited to become active participants. Clearly stated expectations help each child see his role within the classroom. For example, in our classrooms each child knows that he is to work so he does not interfere with the progress of others and that he must do some reading, math and writing each day.

Why do children's interests play such a major role in the curriculum?

The major source of motivation in the open classroom is the child rather than the teacher. The child's interest is the starting point for many activities, and investigations. For example, the child's self-selection of books in our individualized approach to reading is an important motivational factor. It serves to facilitate comprehension as well as to stimulate reading. Self-selection and the power of children's interests applies to the other areas of the curriculum as well.

Why are children involved in planning their daily program?

Children are involved in planning their daily program to give them a feeling of direction and purpose as well as a commitment to specific goals. Daily planning gives children practice in making important decisions, setting priorities and organizing time. The teacher guides the child in this process and helps him to follow through responsibly.

How are basic skills approached?

A child is introduced to new skills when he is ready to benefit from such instruction and when opportunities arise for applying these skills. Many opportunities are given for children to use their skills and to reinforce them through practical application. Although some time is spent practicing skills in isolation, our goal is integrating the use of skills into daily activities, thereby giving meaning and purpose to skills development.

How much emphasis is given to creativity, problem solving, understanding and rote learning?

They all play an important part. Each contributes much to the learning of the child and the teacher seeks out opportunities to provide a variety of experiences in these areas. Much of rote, or repetitious learning, results from the child's daily participation in reading, math and writing activities.

Does a child receive a balanced curriculum?

In both traditional and the open classroom all children are exposed to the wide range of the Independence School District curriculum. However, children are exposed to the curriculum in different ways in the different types of classrooms. At any one point of time in the open classroom, the child will be exposed to more curriculum options. The child has a longer amount of time to become comfortable with and to explore any one particular aspect of the curriculum. For example, in science a child might have the opportunity to explore "balancing" throughout the school year while in a traditional classroom the unit on "balancing" might be introduced and covered in a few weeks' or a month's time. It is true that a child will not benefit equally from all areas of the curriculum in both open and traditional classrooms. In the open classroom the child might not benefit fully from a particular work area because of choice, lack of interest or lack of confidence. In the traditional classroom a child also may not benefit because of lack of interest and confidence, or because of inattentiveness or undue repetition.

Therefore, in both types of classrooms children will be different.

What happens to the child who tends to avoid work and responsibility? How will he learn?

The child who avoids work and responsibility will have diffi-culty in any learning situation. The teacher in the open classroom will focus on the child and seek opportunities to involve the child in areas of his interest. The teacher provides more direction for this child in order to help him connect his interest to skills and concept development and to broaden his participation to many kinds of activities. The teacher encourages the child to accept more responsibility as he becomes more aware of his role in the learning process.

Can all children function in an open classroom?

The vast majority of children can function well in an open class-room. However, there is a small percentage of children who because of a particular learning disability or personal trait will function better in a situation where there is less choice and more teacher direction. Certainly there is no one situation which is best for all children.

How does a child learn self-discipline and responsibility in an open classroom?

Children develop self-discipline when they are given reasonable rights and responsibilities and when they are encouraged to learn from their errors. Children also develop self-discipline when they are actively involved in learning activities and encouraged to set personal standards. By living and working in this open way, children see that their actions have consequences and are helped to learn to be responsible for their actions.

What will happen to the child in the future in a classroom with fewer choices?

Normal healthy children can adapt to new situations in which reasonable demands are made upon them.

Based upon our experiences at Independence School during the past two years, it seems that those children who have participated in an open classroom situation have adapted well to different classrooms with varying degrees of teacher and student choice and direction. Many of the children who have participated in the open classroom have made much progress in understanding adult expectations and accepting adult direction. These are assets in any classroom–traditional or open. Also, children who have learned to participate actively in learning do so in all situations and can make the most of each learning experience.

How can a parent help to make a child's experiences in an open classroom successful?

A parent can be supportive of a child in an open classroom in the same way as in any classroom:

- by valuing a child's school experiences and giving him opportunities to share his feelings as well as his achievements and concerns with you.
- by developing trust between teacher, child and parent.

- by keeping all channels of communication between teacher and parents open–conferring personally with your child's teacher when questions arise or when you have information you wish to share. Remember, your child's teacher is constantly trying to provide a program which will meet the diverse and changing needs of your growing child. A parent plays an important role.

- by recognizing that your child's teacher is concerned with your child's total growth and that he does not make major strides forward in all areas at once. Growth needs time.

How can a visit be arranged? How can I get the most from my visit?

Parents are encouraged to visit and participate in the activities of the open unit. Visitations may be arranged by contacting the school secretary. A parent who visits to share his or her child's school experience contributes much to the child's good feeling about school.

Visitors who actively participate in unit activities gain so much more than the visitor who tries to be a "fly on the wall." In fact, the visitor who remains an idle bystander most often conveys a disinterest and lack of understanding to those around him. Visitors should feel free to ask the teachers how they may participate during their visit.

Are there opportunities for parents to assist in the open unit?

Although this has not been explored by the staff as of yet, there should be opportunities for parents to actively assist in the classroom on an ongoing basis. We intend to explore this more at our parent meetings. If you feel you may be able to assist in the class-room, please communicate this to your child's teacher or to the principal. We welcome your assistance and participation in your child's school.

Appendix II

Attributes of Focused Small Group Instruction

at The Learning Alternative Jerusalem, Israel, 1986-2004

1. CHILD CENTERED TEACHERS: caring, experienced, and well trained.

2. ENROLLMENT BY CHOICE: participation by 3rd thru 8th grade students who were motivated to improve their English. **Time and energy** were not wasted by forcing children to learn something they were neither interested in nor ready to vigorously pursue **at a specific point in time.**

3. SMALL GROUPS OF 5: where hardly a moment was devoted to disciplining individual children or the group.

4. TAILORED INSTRUCTION: As children were grouped by levels of English, the instruction was at an appropriate level (neither "under" nor "overwhelming") and the teacher was able to tailor the pace and introduction of new content to the 5 participants. Furthermore, the teacher was able to select materials that suited their specific interests, thus spurring on the children's motivation.

5. NO NEED FOR TESTING: Time wasn't wasted on testing; the teacher could observe each child's achievement first hand through-

out the hour and the year. Children could sense their own progress, while the teacher encouraged the child with individual positive comments and observations.

6. HOMEWORK FOR REINFORCEMENT: Approximately 15-20 minutes of required homework was given for the following week to provide continuity and reinforcement; in addition, once the children began reading independently, almost every child requested a second book from our extensive paperback library for their reading enjoyment at home (in English, their second language; not in their mother tongue of Hebrew).

7. GRADING—R U Joking? When children very infrequently asked about grades, which appeared to be a carry over from their public school experience, the teacher would point jokingly to his or her own head and indicate that what they learned is in their heads, not in a notebook or in a grade.

8. INCORPORATION OF LEARNING GAMES: Approximately a quarter of the 60 minute hour was used to play a creative learning game that further enhanced the child's motivation to learn English. Every child was a winner as the games were played in a cooperative manner—often the small group was a team playing against the teacher or the clock. Failure and put-downs have no part in such a cooperative learning scheme.

9. FOSTERING FRIENDSHIPS: Friendships within the group of 5 were begun and/or naturally flourished as an outgrowth of the weekly small group meetings.

NOTE:

We were never able to accommodate the long waiting list of students eager to enroll in our English center as it had a reputation as a place where students studied in a friendly learning environment and where they were proud of their accomplishments and their ability to communicate well in English.

Endnotes

1. For a comprehensive study of the Project Concern program in the Hartford Metropolitan Area, please refer to R. Crain, R. L. Miller, J. A. Hawes, and J. R. Peichert, "Finding Niches: Desegregated Students Sixteen Years Later." In Final Report on the Educational Outcomes of Project Concern, Hartford, Connecticut. New York: Institute for Urban and Minority Education, Teachers College, Columbia University, 1992. ERIC Document Reproduction Service No. ED 396 035. (Thanks to Amy W., former Independence School student, for bringing this study to my attention.)

2. W. James Popham, Ed.D., *Testing! Testing!: What Every Parent Should Know About School Tests.* Boston: Allyn and Bacon, 2000. Special attention should be given to chapter 3: The Misuse of Standardized Test Scores as Indicators of Educational Effectiveness and chapter 11: The Pressure to Improve Test Scores–and Its Consequences.

3. Banesh Hoffman, *The Tyranny of Testing,* New York: The Crowell-Collier Press, 1962.

4. Linda Darling-Hammond, *The Right to Learn: A Blueprint for Creating Schools That Work,* San Francisco: Jossey-Bass, John Wiley & Sons, Inc., 1997, p.43.

5. William G. Ouchi with Lydia G. Segal, *Making Schools Work: A Revolutionary Plan to Get Your Children the Education They Need,* New York: Simon & Schuster, 2003, pp. 57-58.

6. Darling-Hammond, p. 67.

7. Carl R. Rogers, *Freedom to Learn for the 80s,* Columbus: Charles E. Merrill Publishing Company, 1983, p. 307.

8. Richard C. Allen, Pastor. Eulogy in memory of Rosina Housley, January 25, 1994.

9. Foster, Car and Back, J. "A Neighborhood School Board: Its Infancy, Its Crises, Its Growth." Education, 95 (Winter 1974): pp. 145-162.

10. Bill and Melinda Gates Foundation, E-Mail Newsletter Announcement: "$51 Million Grant from the Bill & Melinda Gates Foundation to Support Small Dynamic High Schools to Boost Student Achievement," September 17, 2003. Accessed at http://www.gatesfoundation.org/UnitedStates/Education/TransformingHighSchools/Announcements/Announce-030917.htm

11. Linda Darling-Hammond, "'From Separate but Equal' to 'No Child Left Behind': The Collision of New Standards and Old Inequalities." In *Many Children Left Behind: How the No Child Left Behind Act is Damaging Our Children and Our Schools,* edited by Deborah Meier and George Wood. Boston: Beacon Press, 2004.

12. Accessed at www.lifescied.org/cgi/content/abstract/3/2/131